POWER TO ELECT

The Case for
Proportional Representation

POWER TO ELECT

The Case for
Proportional Representation

ENID LAKEMAN

Heinemann : London

William Heinemann Ltd
10 Upper Grosvenor Street,
London W1X 9PA
LONDON MELBOURNE TORONTO
JOHANNESBURG AUCKLAND

SBN: 434 40220 6

Figures 10, 11, 13, 14 & 16 with kind
permission of Nomos Verlagsgesellschaft,
Taken from the work *Das Wahlrecht der Neun –
Wahlsysteme in der Europäischen Gemeinschaft*
edited by Sasse, Christoph, Georgel, Jacques,
Hand, Geoffrey J, 2979, 301 S, DM 38

Filmset by Northumberland Press Ltd,
Gateshead, Tyne and Wear
Printed and bound in Great Britain by
Richard Clay (The Chaucer Press) Ltd, Bungay, Suffolk

Contents

Glossary

ABSOLUTE MAJORITY. More than half the total number of votes cast.

ADDITIONAL MEMBER SYSTEMS (AMS). Electoral systems in which part of a parliament is elected from single-member constituencies and other members are added in such a way as to make each party's total seats as nearly as possible proportional to the number of voters supporting it.

ALTERNATIVE VOTE. A method of securing the election of one person by an absolute majority. Voters number candidates in their order of preference. If no one candidate has half the first-preference votes or more, the one with the fewest votes is excluded and each of his votes is transferred to the candidate marked by that voter as his next preference among those who remain. This is repeated, if necessary, until some one candidate has more votes than all other remaining candidates combined.

APPARENTEMENT. Under party list systems, an arrangement whereby two or more parties are permitted to declare themselves in alliance and to have seats allocated on the basis of their combined votes.

CONTINUING CANDIDATE. In a single transferable vote count, any candidate who, at the relevant stage, is still in the running – neither already elected nor eliminated.

CUMULATIVE VOTE. Each elector has several votes and may give more than one of these to the same candidate.

D'HONDT RULE. A method of calculation designed to ensure that the average number of votes needed to elect a candidate is as nearly as possible the same for all parties. See also HIGHEST AVERAGE.

ELECTORAL COLLEGE. A body of people chosen to elect in their turn another body or person, e.g. the president of the USA or of Finland.

ELIMINATION or EXCLUSION. In a single transferable vote election, a candidate who has so few votes as to be without any further hope of election is excluded from all remaining stages of the count, his votes being transferred to his supporters' next available preferences.

EXHAUSTIVE BALLOT. When no one candidate for a single seat has polled half the votes or more, the candidate with the fewest votes is excluded and a new vote is taken among those who remain. This is repeated, if necessary, until some one candidate has more votes than all his remaining opponents combined. See also SECOND BALLOT and ALTERNATIVE VOTE.

HIGHEST AVERAGE. A method of calculating a party's seats in proportion to its votes. See D'HONDT RULE.

LIMITED VOTE. Several representatives are elected together and each voter may vote X for some specified number of candidates smaller than the number to be elected.

MINORITY VOTE. A person is said to be elected on a minority vote if he has received fewer votes than his two or more opponents combined.

MULTIPLE-X VOTING. Several representatives are elected together and each voter may vote X for that number (or up to that number) of candidates.

NEXT AVAILABLE PREFERENCE. The candidate marked by a voter as his next preference among the continuing candidates.

NON-TRANSFERABLE VOTE. In a single transferable vote election, a vote which cannot be transferred from one candidate to another because the voter has not indicated any further preference.

PARTY LIST PR. A form of proportional representation which depends on casting a vote for a list of candidates submitted by a party.

PLUMPING. Recording a vote for one candidate only in an election in which the voter is permitted to record votes, or preferences, for more than one candidate.

PLURALITY. Relative majority.

POINTS SYSTEM. The voter awards a certain number of points to the candidate he most wants to elect, a smaller number of points to his second preference and so on. The candidate(s) with the highest total(s) of points is/are elected.

PROPORTIONAL REPRESENTATION. Any electoral system designed to give political parties, or other groups, a number of seats proportional to the votes cast for them.

QUOTA. The minimum number of votes required to ensure the election of one representative.

HARE QUOTA. The total number of valid votes cast divided by the number of seats to be filled.

DROOP QUOTA. The total number of valid votes is divided by one more than the number of seats to be filled and 1 (or 0.01 if working to two places of decimals) is added to the result.

RELATIVE MAJORITY. The number of votes by which the votes for the candidate with the most support exceed those for the candidate next in order of votes.

SECOND BALLOT. A second election held to determine the final result when the first has given no one candidate half the total votes or more.

SINGLE NON-TRANSFERABLE VOTE. Each voter has one vote, regardless of how many places have to be filled. That vote is given to one candidate and cannot be transferred to any other.

SINGLE TRANSFERABLE VOTE (STV). A system of election in which each voter has one vote, which is given in the first instance to the candidate the voter most wants to elect but can be transferred, on the voter's instructions, from a candidate it cannot help to elect to one that it can help. When used to elect several representatives together, each by a quota, it gives PROPORTIONAL REPRESENTATION of whatever political parties or other groups exist among the electorate.

SURPLUS. The number of votes by which the votes of a successful candidate exceed the quota.

Introduction

Gradually, since the 1960's, my faith in the natural aptitude of the British to govern themselves has been eroded.... Where are the great parties which made politics in this country a serious and mature affair? ... Has one to include Great Britain in the list of ineffective or even unstable democracies whose evolution is an object of interest and worry among students of politics across the world? ... Who would have thought, 20 years ago, that Britain would cease to be a political model and become an object of puzzlement?

Professor Jean Blondel, *The Times*, 15 August 1980

Many British people will agree with this French critic. We do not despair of democracy, we certainly would not welcome anyone seeking to substitute a dictatorship, whether of Left or Right, but we no longer feel confident in boasting of our institutions as a model to the world. Somewhere, something is wrong. What?

In May 1979 the British people elected a new government. In May 1980 trade unions called a 'day of action' in protest against government policies which had been clearly foreshadowed in its election programme. True, that call was by no means massively supported, but protests continued. When strikes in Poland forced drastic changes in government policy, there were demands that British workers do likewise – that is, the British government, a product of our admired democratic system, was equated with the Polish government whose pretensions to any legitimacy conferred on it by the people would be ridiculed by most of those same protesters.

Let us examine that protest. Is it a claim that, although a certain policy has been accepted by a majority of the nation, those who consider it mistaken are entitled to overturn it by force? Few would openly argue this and they would attract little sympathy, but their case is much more plausible, for our elections afford no proof that our government's actions are supported by a majority of the voters, let alone of the entire electorate. Opponents of the government that came to power in 1979 can quite legitimately argue that they did not vote for it and that only 44 people did so for every 56 who voted for something else. (How many of the 56 are bitterly opposed to the government and how many accept it as a reasonable second best cannot be deduced from the election result.)

Conservatives	13,697,753		43.9%
Labour	11,506,741		
Liberal	4,305,324	17,524,526	56.1%
Others	1,712,461		

Unfortunately for that argument, however, the previous government, of opposite complexion, came to power with even less support – 39 per cent of those voting – and it had no hesitation in claiming its right to rule. Those who accept a system which puts one minority in power must accept the same system when it puts a different minority in power. Those who are entitled to protest are those who attack the system itself and seek to replace it with one that will ensure government by the majority.

Signs abound that the number of such people is large and growing. Discontent with the system has shown itself in decreasing turnout in elections, a much larger decrease in votes for the two parties with immediate prospects of forming the government, defections of politicians from those parties, a tendency for the public spirited to join pressure groups for specific objects rather than the parties, and a series of public opinion polls which consistently show a majority of about two to one for changing the way in which we elect the House of Commons. Typical of these polls is one by Opinion Research and Communication published in *The Times* of 17 January 1980:

'Do you think it would be a good idea or a bad idea if a new system of voting were brought in?

	Good idea	Bad idea	Don't know
(a) So that the number of seats a party wins in an election is in proportion to the number of votes it gets in an election	72	13	15

	Good idea	Bad idea	Don't know
(b) Which would make it more difficult for the largest party in parliament to do what it wants without taking any notice of what the other parties want	45	35	20
(c) Which would only make it possible for one party to· form a government after an election if it had won half or more of the votes	52	26	22

'Analysed by party the Liberals, not unexpectedly, are more in favour of electoral reform, but the differences are not great. In general the unease cuts across parties and there would be a general welcome among voters for some sign that political power equated more fairly with votes cast.'

Discontent does not relate only to the misrepresentation of the parties. Other groups are becoming restive. Why has the female half of the British population only 19 MPs against 616 men? Why are there no black MPs? There is growing dislike of 'yah-boo politics', of parliamentary debates in which the speeches are a ritual that changes nobody's vote, of creaking machinery that allows a government proposal manifestly not wanted by the majority of MPs to be defeated only by a House of Lords vote followed by a filibuster that kept the Commons up all night and cancelled other important business*, of unedifying disputes within a party over the selection, by perhaps some 50 people, of a candidate who, if elected, purports to represent a thousand times that number of electors. People whose MP is on the left of his party may wish they had a right-winger or vice versa but can do nothing about it; they may heartily dislike some item in the policy of the party whose candidate they have voted for, but they are nevertheless counted as having given a 'mandate' for this along with everything else in the party's manifesto. Those electors who find one such item unacceptable and feel more agreement on that point with some other party have no means of expressing this, and an MP who behaves in accordance with that conviction is likely to be treated as a traitor to his party. If people of different parties wish to co-operate for some purpose, they find great obstacles in their way. Industrialists and others who need to plan ahead cannot do so with confidence beyond the next election, since a change of the party in power may transform the conditions under which they

* Housing Bill, 6 August 1980.

have to work – whether or not there is evidence of public demand for that change.

A century ago, reversals of policy every few years may have mattered less; now that governments meddle in every aspect of our daily lives, there is a crying need for more stability. We need a reform that will give legislation acceptable to the majority of the nation and leave it unchanged until such time as the majority are persuaded to change their minds.

1
What's Going Wrong?

A surge of public concern about parliamentary elections was set off by the February 1974 result. Not only was the under-representation of the third party much more extreme than usual (2 per cent of the seats for 19 per cent of the votes) but no foundation was left for the argument that we must put up with this kind of thing for the sake of "strong government". There was no "strong government". The party with the most votes lost, no one party had a parliamentary majority, and it was several days before it became clear which would form the government. That government called a new election after only seven months.

Discontent continued to increase. On the Conservative side industrialists felt themselves threatened by socialist measures for which there was no evidence of majority popular demand, while after the 1979 election it was Labour people who resented destruction of some of their party's work and vowed revenge at the first opportunity. Within the parties, dissension spread and accusations of a take-over by extremists multiplied. The case of the MP for Newham North East became a *cause célèbre*, dragging on for months while the General Management Committee of his constituency party voted first one way then another on whether he should continue to represent the constituency or not. The decision was swayed by half a dozen people allegedly imported from outside. The attention of the electors was drawn to the fact that the twenty-two thousand of them who had voted for the right-wing Reg Prentice had no means of either re-electing or dismissing him but were in the hands of a tiny minority. Numerous other examples, by no means confined to one party, have continued to produce newspaper headlines such as "candidate choice row". They have become more conspicuous owing to the Labour party's new rule that every MP must face re-selection by his constituency party. Some have been re-selected by a margin so large that it may reasonably be thought to indicate general support (19 votes to 3 in Oldham East), but others have barely survived (18 to 16 in Dunbartonshire West) and others equally narrowly failed (in Birmingham, Ladywood, after a prolonged dispute over the nomination procedure, the sitting MP lost by what was reported as a very small margin).

A trickle of people leaving the party to which they had been long attached explained their action by words to the effect that 'I haven't left the party; the party has left me' – that is, the party had moved away from the policies or attitudes that originally attracted them and they despaired of ever being able to bring it back to them. They still held the same beliefs but had lost the medium for their expression.

Defection on a much larger scale was talked of in 1980 and became a fact with the formation of the Social Democratic party in 1981. This was in origin a right-wing Labour party but clearly had much in common with the Liberals and soon attracted recruits also from the Conservatives and from people not previously active in politics. It entered the electoral arena with a borough council by-election in the Bishop's Ward of Lambeth, a Social Democrat and a Liberal supporting one another in a contest for a double vacancy. Both were elected, with a 3 to 2 majority over Labour in a supposedly impregnable Labour ward, and on the same day other gains were registered in various parts of the country. The Liberals had already been gaining council seats in considerable numbers, but the alliance soon demonstrated its ability to do much better. Public opinion polls showed support for the alliance exceeding the total for the two parties separately, and that support rose steadily. Three parliamentary by-elections followed, with one of the SDP founders, Roy Jenkins, narrowly failing to overturn a 10,274 Labour majority in Warrington, Bill Pitt in Croydon North West turning a Conservative majority of 3,769 over Labour into a 3,254 majority for the Liberal, and Shirley Williams romping home in the 'safe' Conservative seat of Crosby. All the time, local council gains continued.

During the preceding twenty years there had been some equally startling Liberal gains, but these had failed to herald any great or lasting change in the pattern of alternating Conservative and Labour governments with other parties playing only a minor part. The 1981 situation was different. Actual votes and public opinion polls agreed in showing that hardly any Conservative or Labour seat could any longer be considered safe, and it made no difference whether the attacking candidate was Liberal or Social Democrat, famous and popular or obscure, what type of constituency was involved or in what part of the country. There was solid evidence of widespread popular welcome for an opportunity to break away from the political pattern that had been taken for granted for so many years. A substantial proportion of those joining the new party and working in by-elections were people who had never previously been active in politics, and – after a long period when even Cabinet ministers had been unable to fill a small room – election meetings were crowded out. That change at least should be welcomed by all democrats, of whatever party.

Moreover, the change was not limited to the emergence of a new party with large popular support; the two that had for so long been the largest were not only shrinking but showing signs of disintegration. The defection of Labour right-wingers did not leave a united party of the left. On the contrary, factions among those who remained were even more conspicuous than before. On the Conservative side, dissatisfaction with the leader's policies was not only openly expressed but in some cases carried to the length of abstaining in a division or even voting with the opposition. There is evidently a growing tendency to reject what was always a ridiculous pretence – that a political party is a monolith which must be supported or opposed in its entirety. People are ready for a change that will reflect more adequately the infinite variety of opinion.

This development also improved greatly the prospect of reform in Britain's electoral system. The Liberals had been pledged to this for many years, and the Social Democrats agreed that it was a top priority. If the voting pattern continued as at the end of 1981, they would certainly be in a position to implement that promise, and the landslide which those votes would produce should be a powerful incentive to the other parties to consider seriously a change that would save for them their proportional share of the seats. Both by-election results and opinion polls gave the Liberal/Social Democrat Alliance between 40 and 50 per cent of the votes, which, with the other two parties more or less equal, would give it something like 500 of the 635 seats.

On the Alliance side, the need for reform is equally great, though for a rather different reason. For them, it should be evident that there is great need for the voters to choose persons to represent them, not just parties. The original 'gang of four' were obliged to make the painful break with the Labour party to which they had for so long been attached, because only by forming a new party could they give voters the chance of supporting the kind of policies they thought necessary. In the 1979 election it was already evident that Labour candidates Tony Benn and Shirley Williams stood for very different things, but anyone wanting a Labour government had no option but to vote for the one if he happened to live in Bristol South East, for the other if he lived in Stevenage. If voters had been free to choose between Labour candidates of both types, the break might never have been necessary. Having made the break, the Social Democrats realized that they had much in common with the Liberals, and that if they were to have any chance of winning the next election they must avoid splitting the votes of those occupying that common ground. It was therefore necessary to ensure that only one of those parties contested any one seat. No party likes to have to stand down for another (especially if it has memories of the 1931 election) and even in the selection of candidates for the three 1981 by-elections there was some friction. In anticipation of the general election (in 1984 or earlier), the two parties set up joint machinery to reach agreement on which of them should fight which seats, also joint committees to arrive at agreed policies on the widest possible range of subjects. It would be of great advantage to the Alliance if the electoral system were such as to allow any number of Liberal and Social Democrat candidates, without risk of splitting the vote, and leave to the voters the decision as to which of them should be elected.

Even if it proves possible to arrive at amicable arrangements on all these matters, there is, under the present X-vote system, no way in which a voter can show whether he approves of them or not. He gives his X to a Liberal and there is no means of knowing whether he does so joyfully or with regret that the candidate is not a Social Democrat. Or vice versa. We cannot tell whether he welcomes the Alliance or supports only the one party and wants to have nothing to do with the other. The X implies total approval of one party and total disapproval of all others, and is clearly unsuitable for a situation in which voters reject that as an adequate expression of their views.

All this coincided with another source of irritation, the periodical revision of parliamentary constituencies. To prevent gross disparity of electorate between one single-member constituency and another, it is necessary to re-draw boundaries every few years to correspond with movements of population and the way in which this is done can affect substantially the result of a general election. Although in general British boundary commissioners are trusted to carry out their work impartially, with no deliberate intent to favour one party or another, they cannot avoid doing so unintentionally, and appeals against their recommendations are sometimes bitter. The Labour government of 1966–70 was charged with dishonesty because it postponed, until after the 1970 election, implementation of a redistribution which abolished a number of Labour-held constituencies of excessively small size. Right or wrong, this postponement was understandable, since those small constituencies made up for the handicap Labour suffered from the concentration of its strength in certain places. Far more Labour than Conservative votes were wasted in piling up huge majorities. In any redistribution, party workers dislike having to adjust themselves to new areas, many MPs find their seats disappearing under them, and many electors have their geographical and personal ties broken. In the 1970 redistribution, the over-sized South East Essex constituency was reduced to normal size by having part removed and assigned to Maldon – from which it was separated by a river without a bridge! Very similar is the proposal in the 1981

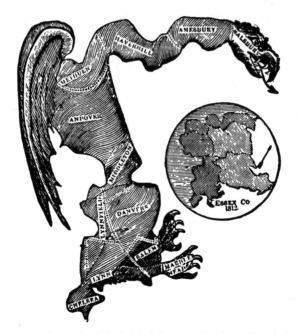

Figure 1 Facsimile of the Original Gerrymander, from a broadside

redistribution to bring the island of Anglesey up to standard electorate by adding to it the mainland town of Bangor. Inland, two Welsh valleys are proposed to be joined although there is no road over the mountains between them. The word gerrymander comes from the activities of Governor Gerry of Massachusetts (1811), who, to give maximum advantage to his party, drew a constituency of salamander-like shape described by an opponent as a 'gerrymander'.

Some equally grotesque shapes have been produced without fraudulent intent, as part of honest efforts to equalize electorates. For instance, part of the 1981 proposals in Kent is a long, narrow constituency to be called Mid Kent. This has no through roads and includes parts of two boroughs, Rochester and Maidstone. Three quarters of the Maidstone borough area are included in the Maidstone parliamentary constituency, but a large part of the town's shopping centre and one of its two railway stations are cut off and placed in Mid Kent.

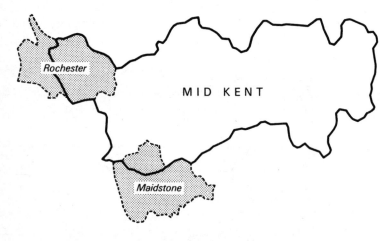

Figure 2

It would be "sixteen miles long, seldom more than two miles wide with no through roads and at one point narrowing to a neck less than a quarter mile across".*

If there seems to be no other way of avoiding such obvious injustice as 23,678 electors in Newcastle upon Tyne Central having the same representation as 104,375 electors in Bromsgrove and Redditch (1979

* *The Guardian*, 27 July 1981.

election), people will put up with such things, but a growing number are now becoming aware that there is a better way.

Revolt against the existing system arises for many different reasons, and may be strengthened by the extension of the franchise to eighteen-year-olds. Older people may be inclined to vote by custom, under a system that they take for granted. Young people with their first vote may be disappointed to find that it has so little effect – that perhaps there was no candidate showing real concern for the matters of real interest to them – and that if there was such a candidate their vote for him, as likely as not, failed to elect him. Many of them lose interest, or divert their interest to something which seems of more practical effect – or, worse, to violent rebellion. Some join the ranks of those who are examining critically our political institutions and seeking to improve them.

2

Palliatives

Among the many features of British parliamentary elections which can be criticized, the most obvious is the very uncertain relation between a party's support in the country and the number of seats it wins. As the graphs in Figure 3 show, the commonest effect is to exaggerate the representation of the party with the most votes. Hence, while the popularity of the two largest parties waxes and wanes over a relatively narrow range, the changes in their representation are much greater. While no single party since 1906 has secured the support of more than half the voters, usually one party has had a majority in the House of Commons. The third party is consistently under-represented, and indeed it was the fate of the Liberal party in the Febuary 1974 election which triggered off a surge of protest – by no means confined to Liberals. The party had nearly trebled its vote, to over half that for either of its two larger rivals, yet won only 14 seats compared with their 301 and 297; this struck large numbers of people as outrageous. Another feature of the same election was less widely noticed: that the party with the most votes lost.

	votes polled	*seats won*
Conservative	11,966,481	287
Labour	11,661,657	301

This has happened before, notably in 1951, when Labour increased its support to the highest level it has ever reached but was thrown out of office.

	votes polled	*seats won*
Labour	13,948,385	295
Conservative	13,724,418	317 + 4 uncontested

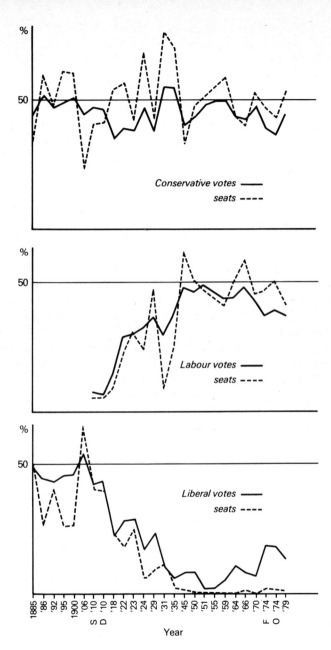

Figure 3

Some people make light of such anomalies, treating them as of little practical importance. One party may get more than its fair share of power in one election, but never mind; the 'swing of the pendulum' will give the opposition its turn next time. This is to ignore the fact that the actions of an unrepresentative legislature may be irreversible. The most obvious example of a lasting effect on a country's history is in South Africa, where the Nationalists came to power in 1948 against the votes of the majority.* Our own country's history has been gravely affected for the worse by at least two anomalies of opposite kinds. Gladstone fought the 1886 election on the issue of Irish Home Rule. The votes cast for the Gladstonian Liberal and Irish Nationalist candidates on the one hand, and for Conservatives and Liberal Unionists on the other, were nearly equal, and if allowance is made for uncontested constituencies the former were probably in a small majority.† Yet, although no single MP was elected on a minority vote, the opponents of Home Rule got a parliamentary majority of 104 seats. This appeared to be a crushing defeat for Gladstone's policy and caused discussion of it to be shelved for many years. Failure to agree on moderate reform then stored up trouble for future generations.

Harm done by inflated power for a majority occurred in the 1930's. Most of the Labour and Liberal opposition and many Conservatives viewed with increasing alarm the "National" government's policy of appeasement towards Hitler and Mussolini, and there was revolt against it by Churchill and a score of other Conservative MPs. The distinguished rebels, however, had no effect, for even if they had all crossed the floor they could have made only a small dent in the government's majority of over 200 seats. If that majority had been only the 40 or so corresponding to its popular support in the 1935 election, the rebels could have forced a reconsideration of foreign policy before it was too late.

Besides the exaggeration of change from one election to the next, there is another unfortunate effect: exaggeration of the difference between one part of the country and another. When Mrs Thatcher was elected leader of the Conservative party, she told her followers that 'What we have to do is to get more votes in the north of England'. But the votes cast in the election preceding this were:

* See pp 21, 159. The United Party had all the 17 majorities over 4,025; the Nationalists 28 out of the 40 majorities under 1,000.

† See J. Rooke Corbett, Manchester Statistical Society, *Transactions*, 12 December 1906.

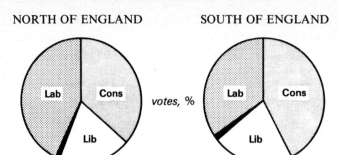

NORTH OF ENGLAND   SOUTH OF ENGLAND

votes, %

The difference is hardly so striking as to justify the high priority given by Mrs Thatcher to that objective. The importance she attached to it arose from the false impression created by the *seats won* in the two halves of England:

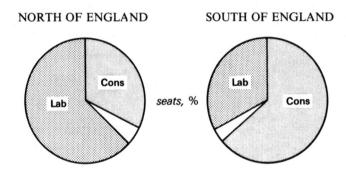

NORTH OF ENGLAND   SOUTH OF ENGLAND

seats, %

The Conservatives already had plenty of votes in the north; the trouble was that those in the industrial cities elected nobody. Labour had plenty of votes in the south, but outside London hardly any of them elected an MP.

Other leaders, under the same or a similar electoral system, have been led to draw false conclusions, sometimes with disastrous consequences. In 1980 Ronald Reagan was elected president of the United States by a ten to one majority of the electoral college. It may be all too easy for him to forget that his place in the hearts of the American people rested only on an insecure 51 per cent of a low poll. When in 1969 proposals for French local government reform secured only 47 per cent of the votes in a referendum, President de Gaulle imagined he had suffered a catastrophic fall in popularity and resigned. He might have reacted very differently, had he remembered that the three to one majority of seats which Gaullist candidates won in the general election a few months before came from a slightly *smaller* share of the votes (44 per cent on the first ballot, 46 on the second).

The exaggeration of the difference between north and south is unhelpful even in a long-united country like Britain. Where unity is a tender plant of recent growth, it can be very dangerous. A conspicuous contemporary example is Canada, where the separatist tendencies of French-speaking Quebec are certainly encouraged by that province being made to appear in the federal parliament as if it had little in common with the English-speaking provinces. The Liberals nearly monopolize the representation of Quebec (74 seats out of 75 for two thirds of the votes), while in the three westernmost provinces they appear not to exist – although in the same (1980) election they polled nearly one quarter of the votes. Historically, the same distortion is recognized to have been a cause of the American civil war: the predominant opinion in the south was in fact shared by many in the north and vice versa, but representation in Congress made the division appear to be absolute*.

Exaggeration of differences between one geographical area and another is particularly dangerous in the case of federations – such as Canada and the USA. Their component parts are by definition more loosely bound than those of a unitary state and can more easily break away. The beginnings of unity in the European Community would be threatened if, for instance, an election to its parliament made France appear to be overwhelmingly Socialist and West Germany overwhelmingly Christian Democrat, or if one member state's representation changed its complexion entirely on the day of an election. Such things would be all too likely if an electoral system like the British were used. Unity at the centre of a federation, combined with substantial autonomy for its parts, calls for political institutions capable of expressing both individuality and shared ideals.

MINORITY MEMBERS

It is sometimes assumed that the anomalies in British election results are due to, or at least greatly increased by, the 'intervention' of third

* See *Unanimous Report of Select Committee on Representative Reform*, presented to the Senate, 2 March 1869.

or fourth parties, causing many MPs to be elected with fewer votes than their two or more opponents combined. It is certainly a fact that many MPs are so elected, the worst instance in 1979 being Belfast North, where the first of seven candidates won with little more than one quarter of the votes (27.6%).

McQuade, J	Dem. U.	11,690
Walker, AC	Off. U.	10,695
O'Hare, P	SDLP	7,823
Dickson, Mrs AL	UPNI	4,220
Cushnahan, J	Alliance	4,120
Lynch, S	Rep. Clubs	1,907
Carr, A	NI Lab.	1,889

There is, however, no consistent relation between the number of MPs elected on a minority vote and the degree of distortion in their parties' representation.

SEATS WON ON A MINORITY VOTE

	Cons	Lab	Lib	others	total
1918	51	12	21	10	94
1922	95	54	17	10	176
1923	96	70	49	1	216
1924	78	31	9	2	120
1929	149	125	40	1	315
1931	21	4	7	1	33
1935	32	17	7	2	58
1945	95	74	2	6	177
1950	106	76	5	0	187
1951	25	14	0	0	39
1955	25	11	1	0	37
1959	47	31	2	0	80
1964	153	72	7	0	232
1966	126	41	11	0	178
1970	68	45	6	3	122
1974 Feb.	234	150	9	15	408
Oct.	224	131	11	14	380
1979	107	82	7	10	206

In all elections since 1918 (when contests with more than two candidates first became the rule rather than the exception) the Conservatives have won the most seats by a minority, even when, as for instance in 1945, they have been badly under-represented. The

Power to Elect

greatest exaggeration of the largest party's representation occurred in 1931 when the number of minority seats was the smallest (33), while the nearest approach to proportional representation of the parties was in 1923 when the number of minority seats was the fifth largest in the period (216). The party with the *second* largest number of votes won the most seats in 1929, when there were 315 minority seats, but also in 1951 when there were only 39. The record number of minority seats for the Conservatives in February 1974 coincided with their defeat by a party with fewer votes. The 1945 election also provides an illustration of the fact that to eliminate election by a minority could make the total result *less* representative. Labour won 62 per cent of all the seats (for 48 per cent of the votes) but, with 59 per cent of the votes, 83 per cent of those in which its candidates had a straight fight with Conservative (or National) candidates only. In the circumstances of that time, Liberals with no candidate of their own tended to vote to defeat the Conservatives, whose government they associated with appeasement of Hitler and with unemployment, so the absence of a third candidate helped to inflate the already excessive Labour majority of seats.

Elections held under the British system and involving only two parties are rare, but they include examples both of gross over-representation of the larger party and of its defeat. In Jamaica in 1976 the People's National Party won 57 per cent of the votes and 78 per cent of the seats, and four years later this was reversed to the benefit of the Jamaica Labour Party. In South Africa, the Nationalists came to power in 1948 in an election where every member was elected by a clear majority, but a 5-to-4 vote for continuance of the United Party government resulted in a 5-to-4 majority of the contested seats for the Nationalists.

Thus, to eliminate election of one person by a minority of the votes cast gives no guarantee of a fair result in the election of a parliament. Nevertheless, it is an anomaly very obvious to the voters concerned and it is not tolerated by any of the British parties when electing its leader. Means of ensuring election with the consent of at least half the people voting are all variations on the basic idea that when there is a result like that in Belfast North (p 13) the voters supporting candidates who clearly cannot be elected should be asked whether they wish to confirm the election of the leading candidate or to substitute one of his rivals. That is, they are asked to vote again. There are many variations of this. In the **exhaustive ballot** candidates are eliminated one by one from the bottom until

British voting system.   A 'straight fight' everywhere.

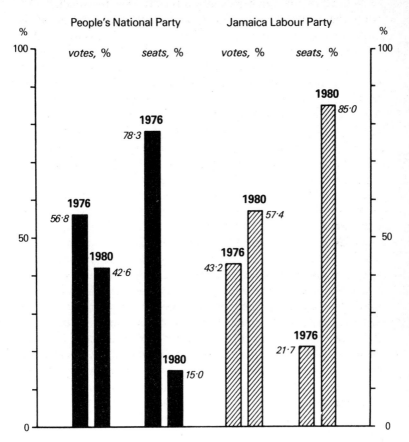

Figure 4 "Landslide" in Jamaica

only two are left or one has more votes than his two or more
opponents combined. Clearly this can be a lengthy process, convenient when voting is by show of hands in a meeting but costly in
time and money when ballot papers have to be circulated to large
numbers of people. It used to be common in British trade unions
but has now generally been superseded by the far more expeditious
alternative vote (see p 18). The **second ballot** (which used to be
common in continental Europe but for the election of members of
parliament is now confined to France) also has variations. In France

up to the Second World War, not only could all candidates in the
first ballot compete again in the second but new candidates could
appear. The second ballot being final – whether any one candidate
received more than half the votes or not – it was quite common for
a Deputy to be elected by a minority. When the system was restored
in 1958, candidature in the second ballot was restricted to those
who had polled at least 5 per cent of the total votes in the first; this
was later raised to 10 per cent and in the 1978 election to 12½ per
cent. This 1978 election was the first in which each Deputy was
elected by a clear majority. In the election of the French president
(by direct popular vote) the second ballot is now restricted to the
two candidates leading on the first.

Although it is less common than it once was to hear France held
up as an example of instability arising from proportional representation, it does still happen – because neither of Britain's two largest
political parties has ever drawn its members' attention to the
absurdity of this allegation. It is like attacking private enterprise on
account of imperfections in the Post Office. The misconception
appears to arise from the idea that the unproportional results of
British elections arise from a third party "splitting the vote"; it is
assumed that because the second ballot gets rid of this (more or
less) the result must be proportional. It may therefore be worth
while to examine in some detail the two most recent general elections
for the French Assembly (1978 and 1981), in each of which every
member was elected by a clear majority. It is true that there was in
each case another factor making for unfair results – gross disparity
in electorates between different constituencies – but the same out
of date boundaries can hardly have favoured the Right in one election
and the Left in the next.

Classifying as best we can the numerous and frequently changing
French parties, we find that there has been a real swing to the left
but that, as so often happens with single-member systems, the result
in terms of seats greatly exaggerates its magnitude. The Left won
the presidency, after vainly attempting this for 23 years, and President Mitterrand promptly called a general election in order to be
able to govern with an Assembly of similar complexion. In this he
succeeded beyond expectation, his Socialist party alone winning a
comfortable majority of all the seats, freeing him from any depend-
ence on the Communists. (He did nevertheless choose to include
four Communists in his cabinet, which one may hope is an indication
that he may give sympathetic consideration to an electoral system

that facilitates co-operation between people of different parties.) The Socialist party gained a great deal of support, nearly doubling its votes but trebling its share of the seats (see figure 5). The exaggeration of the swing arises, just as in Britain, from the number of marginal seats, where a very few voters changing sides may reverse the representation of the entire constituency. In the 1978 election there were 57 Deputies elected with majorities of less than 1 per cent – 28 government and 29 opposition. Therefore a 0.5 per cent swing to the government could have given it 29 extra seats, raising its majority to 150, while the same swing in the opposite direction could reduce the majority from 92 to 36. In the event, the much larger swing naturally affected a much larger number of seats. With a proportional system, it would have meant the gain or loss of only one out of the several seats in a constituency, so could not have been seriously exaggerated.

Instead of the cumbersome machinery of repeated ballots, election by an absolute majority can be secured in a single ballot by the

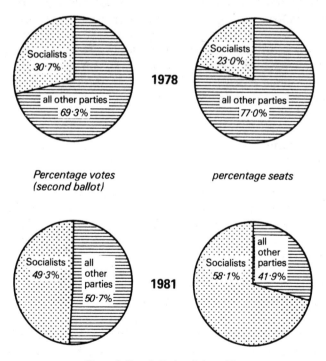

Figure 5 French National Assembly

alternative vote (a somewhat misleading name, since it suggests that only a second choice is involved, while there may actually be many). This simply means that the voter indicates, on his one and only ballot paper, not only which candidate he most favours but also which he would support instead if his favourite could *not* be elected. That is, he numbers in the order of his preference as many of the candidates as he pleases. The "1" votes are counted first, and if any candidate has more than half the total he is declared elected. If not, the candidate with the fewest votes is eliminated and each of his votes is transferred to whichever of the remaining candidates that voter has marked as his next preference. This is repeated if necessary until some one candidate emerges with more votes than all his remaining opponents combined.

This clearly means a great saving of time, and makes unnecessary any limitations on the number of candidates. It would obviate the interminable, and usually fruitless, bargaining that goes on between French parties (especially Socialists and Communists) with a view to pooling their voting strength, for at no stage is there any question of one candidate having to stand down in order to leave a clear run for another, nor need any voter fear that in voting for Party A's candidate he will be supporting a pact with Party B of which he disapproves; if he does think B an acceptable substitute in the event of A failing to be elected, he will vote 2 for B; if not, he will give B only a low preference or none at all.

In general, the alternative vote will give the same final result as the exhaustive ballot, but it is sometimes argued that the latter is preferable because it enables the voter to change his vote in the light of the known wishes of other voters. This is valid only if there is no restriction on the number of candidates standing in the second ballot. For suppose there is a candidate who approaches the position of being everyone's second choice. He may well be more suitable for, say, the position of president than one who is loved by half the voters and hated by the other half, but under the alternative vote he stands no chance of election because he will get few or no first-preference votes and so will be eliminated before having any chance to profit from second preferences. In a second ballot, on the contrary, voters can switch to a compromise candidate, if he is allowed to stand and is not excluded by any limitations such as now apply to French elections. An example of the possibilities of the former French system is the first division of St Etienne in 1936, when the Communist candidate was leading on the first ballot but much behind the total of non-Communist candidates. Three of the latter agreed to withdraw in favour of a compromise candidate (who later became prime minister):

		First ballot	*Second ballot*
Thibaud	Communist	7,081	9,160
Dubreuil	Left Republican	4,542	—
Vernay	Radical Socialist	3,895	—
Besson	Left Independent	3,239	1,029
Robert	Socialist	1,453	3
Pinay	Independent Radical	—	10,861 elected

These possibilities are destroyed if the second ballot is limited to the two candidates leading in the first ballot, as was the case in the French presidential election of 1981. The first ballot result was:

Giscard d'Estaing	8,222,969
Mitterrand	7,505,295
Chirac	5,225,720
Marchais	4,456,979
Lalonde	1,126,282
Laguiller	668,195
Crépeau	642,815
Debré	482,067
Garaud	386,489
Bouchardeau	321,391

Chirac's supporters had made a great effort to get him into second place and therefore into the run-off. Had they succeeded, at Mitterrand's expense, the voters in the second ballot would have had a choice only between two right-wingers, Giscard and Chirac; Mitterrand's Socialists and Marchais's Communists, with any others of the Left, would have had nobody to vote for. The possibility of such an anomaly is even greater in the primary election for New York's mayor in 1977. The result of that primary was:

Koch	180,260
Cuomo	170,573
Beame	163,616
Abzug	150,761
Sutton	131,185
Badillo	99,994
Harnett	13,927

In the French presidential election, at least the second ballot was between two candidates supported by a total of more than half the voters, but in New York it was between Koch and Cuomo, for whom only 39 per cent had voted, leaving out the five wanted by the other 61 per cent. Had candidates been eliminated one by one from the bottom, any one of the leading five might have been the final winner.

The alternative vote is incontestably superior to this limited second ballot, though it may be considered inferior to an open second ballot because it gives no chance of electing a compromise candidate.

Other methods have been proposed which do give a good chance of election to the universal second preference* and these are worth serious consideration when the election of only one person is inescapable (e.g. in the case of a president) but they need not detain those concerned with the election of parliaments, councils or committees, for *no* method of electing only one person at a time can possibly guarantee even that the largest group of voters wins the most seats, let alone any fair representation of other groups.

This is seen in practice, for neither in France (second ballot) nor in Australia (alternative vote) is the representation of the parties any more proportional than it is in Britain. Exaggeration of the largest party's support is usual; for instance in the Australian House of Representatives election of 1977 the Liberal–Country party alliance polled 48 per cent of the votes but won 86 seats against 38 for Labour and none for any other party. Defeat of the party with the most votes also occurs; for instance JFH Wright, President of the Proportional Representation Society of Australia, says† that "Possibly the worst case was the House of Representatives election of 1954, in which the Labour party received over half the first preferences in the contested seats but won fewer seats than the Liberal and Country party coalition".

It is easy to prove theoretically that such things are inevitable under any electoral system that gives the whole representation of a

---

* For details see JR Bainbridge (*Public Administration*, Australia, December 1947, p418), Duncan Black (*Canadian Journal of Economic and Political Science*, May 1949, p 158), *JFS Ross* (*Elections and Electors*, chapters 5 to 7 and *Parliamentary Affairs*, Summer 1953, p 277) and Enid Lakeman (*How Democracies Vote*, 4th edn, p 294) and Steven J Brams, *The Presidential Election Game*, Yale University Press, 1981.

† *The Economist*, 6 September 1965.

constituency to one party. Even if only two parties existed, and even if it were possible to make all constituencies exactly equal in electorate, the result of a general election could be anything between the winning of every seat by a party with only just over half the votes and defeat of a party with far more support.

	constituency I	II	III	total votes	seats won
1. Party A	20,001	20,001	20,001	60,003	3
Party B	20,000	20,000	20,000	60,000	0
	40,001	40,001	40,001		
2. Party A	20,000	20,000	30,000	70,000	1
Party B	20,001	20,001	10,001	50,003	2
	40,001	40,001	40,001		

The reason for such anomalies is that so large a proportion of the votes cast have no effect on the result. In each constituency we can make sure that the majority wins, but the minority – even if only one fewer than the majority – vote in vain. Moreover, there is no possible means of giving any more effect to a huge majority than to a tiny one. A party gets one seat if its candidate polls one more than half the votes; it would get no more than one if he had every vote in the constituency. No remedy is possible if a parliament, or other body, is elected from single-member constituencies.

Such a system also makes the result of an election depend to a high degree on how constituency boundaries are drawn, and offers great scope for their manipulation to favour a particular party. In the second example above, the under-representation of the larger party is caused by the concentration of its strength in constituency III. If the boundaries were altered so as to exchange one quarter of constituency III with one quarter of II and a second quarter with a quarter of I, party B could win all three seats.

Suppose there is a town whose electorate entitles it to three seats and a boundary commission is required to divide it into three equal constituencies. Among the many possible ways of doing this are:

(a) to follow obvious lines of communication, using as boundaries main roads leading to the centre;

(b) to make the three divisions the manufacturing centre, a residential suburb to the north and another to the south.

Suppose parties A and B have voting strengths of 70,000 and

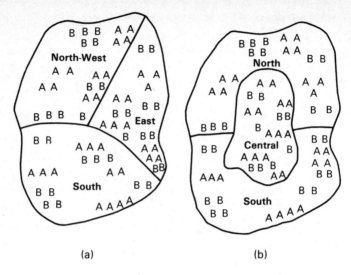

Figure 6

50,003 as in example 2, party A being concentrated in the centre; arrangement (a) will give party A all three seats, arrangement (b) only one.

Either plan might be adopted by a perfectly impartial commission, or might be a deliberate gerrymander on behalf of party B in the first case, B in the second. The possibility of a gerrymander gives rise to suspicion even if there is no real ground for it.

No escape from this is possible with single-member constituencies. Even if no member is elected by a minority, anything up to half the votes in each constituency will be ineffective because cast for losing candidates – the total of these in the 1979 British election was 46 per cent and in the two 1974 elections it reached 51 per cent. In addition, many of those who voted for winning candidates might have stayed at home and the result would have been exactly the same. In South Fylde in 1979 the MP was elected with 45,883 votes, a majority of 32,247 over his nearest rival, so 70 per cent of his supporters made no real contribution to his election. Moreover, many thousands of people (of the largest parties, let alone any others) find their votes ineffective throughout their lives. The worst case is that of a Conservative in South Shields, where neither he nor any of his ancestors since the town was enfranchised by the first Reform Act of 1832 has ever helped to elect an MP. In large areas

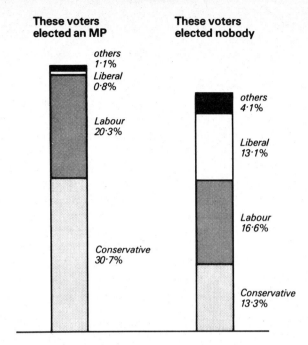

Figure 7 United Kingdom General Election, 1979

of southern England, no Labour supporter has elected an MP since that party was founded.

If several members are elected together, it does become possible to give effect to a much larger proportion of the votes. For example in a 5-member constituency people of up to five different opinions could each elect a representative; if there were two nearly equal parties, the larger could have three seats and the smaller two, while a larger majority could win four seats and near unanimity all five.

However, in Great Britain there are many elections of several representatives together and nothing of this sort happens. On the contrary, where parties are involved the largest of them nearly always takes all the seats. It gets the whole representation of the place concerned, but this is no longer just one seat; it is several. Consequently, the distortions of the single-member system are magnified. Multi-member constituencies are essential for fair representation but are far from sufficient.

For instance, in the latest London borough elections (1978) the result in the Heathfield ward of Richmond was:

Conservative	1,963	Liberal	1,351	Labour	923
candidates	1,959		1,347		866
	1,869		1,318		847

5,791 votes for Conservative candidates elected all three councillors for that ward; 6,652 votes for Liberal or Labour candidates elected nobody. (Another obvious feature of this result is that few people appear to distinguish between one candidate and another of the same party (see figure 8). This will be discussed later – see p 108.)

This pattern is the result of allowing each elector to cast as many votes as there are seats to be filled. If there are 1,869 people whose main concern is to elect Conservative councillors, each of them will vote X for each of that party's three candidates, so each of them will get 1,869 votes (plus any that may be given to them for personal, not party, reasons) and will be elected ahead of the Liberals who get one vote each from 1,318 people. Seats will be shared between two (or more) parties only if a large number of votes are given for personal, not party, reasons, and in the cities this seldom happens.

Multiple-X voting also introduces a hazard which does not exist in single-member constituencies: a candidate may be defeated by the votes of his own supporters. An instance in which this almost certainly did happen was the Queen's Gate ward of Kensington in the same (1978) London borough council elections. The votes for the top four candidates were as follows, with seven other candidates polling only 212 votes or fewer.

Pole	Conservative	1,413	elected
Russell	Conservative	1,318	elected
Crofton	Conservative	1,246	elected
Bach	Ind. Resident	1,075	

The 1,075 people who gave a vote to Bach each had two other votes – 2,150 in all – and if they used these they were necessarily voting *against* Bach. Since Bach was only 171 votes behind the lowest Conservative and only 338 behind the highest, it is practically certain that only a small proportion of Bach's supporters using their second and third votes for Conservative candidates prevented Bach from being in the top three.

This has the further effect of encouraging the growth of organized parties, even where, as in local government, there is an undercurrent of feeling that they are inappropriate. If Bach realizes how it is that

Heathfield Ward, votes

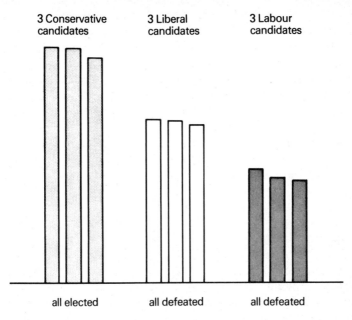

3 Conservative candidates   3 Liberal candidates   3 Labour candidates

all elected   all defeated   all defeated

Figure 8 London Borough of Richmond upon Thames, 1978

Whole Borough

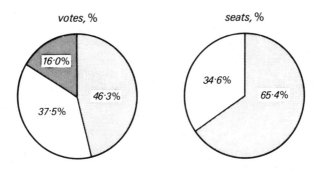

votes, %   seats, %

16·0%   46·3%   37·5%   34·6%   65·4%

Figure 9

he has lost, he will organize his supporters to ensure that it does
not happen in the next election. They may agree either not to use
their second and third votes at all or to use them in a particular
way (e.g. for Pole and Russell, not for Crofton), in which case Bach
will be sure of election. Or they may select two other candidates of
similar opinions to stand with Bach as an Independent Residents
party – in which case all three of them will be elected. (Assuming,
of course, that the behaviour of other voters remains the same.)
Thus, a candidate of an organized party has an immense advantage
over a lone Independent.

Some organizations using multiple-X voting require their electors
to use all their votes. The reasons why they feel "plumping" to be
wrong are obscure; what is clear is that this rule adds to the difficulties
of a candidate such as Bach and increases the risk that the favourite
of the majority may be defeated. In June 1981, the Council on
Foreign Relations in New York held an election whose result so
embarrassed the group that it issued an official statement expressing
alarm. There were nine candidates for eight seats, and the one
candidate not elected was Dr Henry Kissinger. Each voter was
obliged to use all his eight votes. No figures are available to the
public, but it is clear that Kissinger could have been defeated if as
many as three quarters of those voting thought he was the one
candidate above all others who should be elected, while the other
quarter wanted to keep him off. Supposing there were 100 voters,
the result could be:

candidate	votes from anti-Kissinger group	votes from pro-Kissinger group	totals
A	25	71	96
B	25	70	95
C	25	70	95
D	25	68	93
E	25	66	91
F	25	65	90
G	25	60	85
H	25	55	80
K	—	75	75
totals	200	600	800

Such possibilities arise from each voter having as many votes as
there are seats to be filled; hence, systems have been proposed which

reduce that number. The **limited vote** was used in some British parliamentary elections from 1868 to 1880, and Japan elects its parliament by allowing each elector only one vote in a multi-member constituency. This does give a minority a good chance of representation; for instance, in that Queen's Gate election, if 1,246 Conservatives had each had only two votes there is no way in which they could have distributed them so as to give all three Conservative candidates more votes than the 1,075 obtained by the Independent. Also, Bach's supporters would have had only half as many votes available for use against him. However, the result is somewhat uncertain and is open to party manipulation.

In the Birmingham election of 1880, the Liberals won all three seats by efficient organization – knowing their voting strength by a fairly accurate canvass and dividing the votes nearly equally among the three candidates by instructing supporters in one ward to vote for Muntz and Bright, those in another for Muntz and Chamberlain and those in a third for Bright and Chamberlain.

Muntz	Liberal	22,969	Burnaby	Conservative	15,735
Bright	Liberal	20,079	Calthorpe	Conservative	14,208
Chamberlain	Liberal	19,544			
		62,592			29,943
seats		3			0

If fewer people had obeyed instructions, or if the Liberals had overestimated their strength, the party could easily have missed winning that third seat, and could almost have won only one seat to its smaller opponent's two. This had actually happened in Leeds in 1874, when the Liberals rashly ran too many candidates with the following result:

Carter	Liberal	15,390	Wheelhouse	Conservative	14,864
Baines	Liberal	11,850	Tennant	Conservative	13,192
Lees	Liberal	5,994			
		33,234			28,056
seats		1			2

This tends to lead to stagnation, noticeable in Japan which uses the **single non-transferable vote***. Allowing each elector only one vote,

---

* Contrast the single transferable vote, p. 45.

irrespective of the number to be elected, does in practice give nearly proportional representation of the parties, but at the cost of inhibiting a party trying to improve its position and preventing it from giving voters a free choice between different candidates. If, for example, a party already holds one seat and believes its support has increased substantially, it may not dare to try for a second seat lest, by splitting its vote, it loses both.

The Japanese general election of 1976 illustrates both the broadly satisfactory representation of parties and the failure of the system to reflect other opinions.

	candidates	*votes,* %	*seats won*	*seats,* %
Liberal Democrats	319	41.8	249	48.7
Socialists	162	20.7	123	24.1
Komeito	84	10.9	55	10.8
Democratic Socialists	51	6.3	29	5.7
Communists	128	10.4	17	3.3
New Liberals	25	4.2	17	3.3
others	121	5.7	21	4.1
	890	100.0	511	100.0

It will be seen that the result is not far from proportional except in the case of the badly under-represented Communists. They polled almost exactly the same share of the votes as in the previous election (1972) but fell from 38 seats out of 491 to 17 out of 511. This appears to have been due to the emergence of a new party, the New Liberals, which took enough votes from the Communists to destroy their precarious hold on the last seat in many constituencies. The New Liberals, who had split off from the Liberal Democrats and presumably took many votes from them, were very successful for a new party and the backing they got seemed part of a tendency of the Japanese voters to demand a change, not so much in the general party structure as in the people directing it. *The Economist* called the new party a protest against the Liberal Democrats" "stodgy, corrupt and unproductive ways" and the Komeito, whose motto was "clean government", also did well, increasing its vote from 8.5 to 10.9 per cent and its seats from 29 to 55. It is the more regrettable that the system does not give the voters any means of expressing such feelings by choice of candidates within a party. There was a leadership struggle within the largest party, but its grass-roots supporters could not influence its outcome by their votes. Contrast Ireland, see below, p 191.

Another device is the **cumulative vote**, which gives each elector as many votes as there are seats to be filled but allows him to cumulate two of them (or perhaps more than two) on one candidate. This makes it possible for a minority to concentrate its strength on one candidate and thus to secure representation. It also enables a voter to give particular personal support to one candidate without necessarily ignoring all others, and it reduces (but does not eliminate) the danger that a voter may contribute to the defeat of the candidate he most wants to elect.

In the United Kingdom, the cumulative vote was used under the Education Act of 1870 to elect school boards – it being recognized that it was desirable for the opinions of different religious communities to be represented. The system did achieve the representation at least of two main parties and sometimes also an Independent. Usually also their representation was in close proportion to their votes though there were some exceptions; for instance in Tower Hamlets in 1900 the Progressives, with 7,437 votes to the Moderates' 6,199, obtained three seats to the Moderates' one. Other uses include the Illinois state legislature and boards of directors in a number of American companies.

Points systems operate on the same principle, but instead of allowing the voter to decide how many votes to cumulate on whom, it requires him to give a certain specified number of votes to the candidate he most wants, a specified smaller number to the candidate of his second choice and so on. (To do so, the voter simply numbers candidates in the order of his choice.) Objections to this are that the values assigned to first and later choices are arbitrary and that a later choice still counts against an earlier one, though of course to a smaller extent than with equal X's. If the voter is obliged to number all the candidates, thus giving points to some he does not want at all, the result can be as bad as with equal X's.

Thus, all these modifications of multiple-X voting go some way to remove its worst features and to give some representation of both majorities and minorities, but are uncertain in their operation.

The distortion of party representation is the most generally noticed effect of the British electoral system, but elections do not exist for the benefit of the parties. They are a consultation of the people, and the people are sure to have views on many things besides the parties. They do. Not only is there declining support for the two largest parties (who shared about 90 per cent of the votes up to 1970 but were down to 80.8 per cent in 1979) and a proliferation of small ones, there is also evidence of anti-party feeling. Not that this is any new thing. "Politician" has long tended to be a term of abuse, and while the expression "lobby-fodder" is a recent coinage, contempt for the MP who "always voted at my party's call, and never thought of thinking for myself at all" goes back beyond WS Gilbert at least to Burke's time. What is noticeable at the present time is a growing disposition to do something about it. Some members of the Labour party found themselves no longer prepared to preserve party unity by toeing a line with which they disagreed. They broke away as the Social Democrats and – contrary to the usual party isolationism – sought means of collaborating with Liberals to the extent that they had opinions in common. This development has been welcomed by many who felt the existing party structure to be too rigid. Within the parties there are moves to make their organization more democratic – though in the case of Labour there is fierce controversy on whether particular measures proposed will make it more or less democratic. The block vote in trade unions (like the electoral college vote in the USA) is looked on by many as an absurdity, one delegate casting his card vote on behalf of perhaps half a million voters as if they were unanimous, and some recognize this as no different from the MP casting his vote in the name of some 70,000 constituents although probably half or more of them disagree with what he is doing. Much publicized quarrels over the selection of a candidate have drawn attention to the power-lessness of the voters to choose the man or woman they wish to represent them; the party has to select just one candidate in each constituency and in practice this has to be done by some form of committee which is very small compared with the 20,000 or so who will vote for the winning candidate, let alone the entire electorate whom he is supposed to represent. In May 1981 it was decided that the MP for Oldham East should again be his party's candidate in the next election. This was decided by 22 people, voting 19 to 3. The member for Nottingham West was similarly reselected by 22 votes to 13, while those for Bradford North and Birmingham Ladywood were refused re-nomination by 35 to 38 and 18 to 15 votes respectively. At the other extreme we have the exceptional case of a postal ballot of all the local party's paid-up members. This happened in Bournemouth East and Christchurch in 1959, after a long and acrimonious dispute over the Conservative MP, Nigel

Nicolson; the vote was 3,762 to 3,671 against him – a tiny majority of the 7,433 people voting compared with the 28,757 who had voted for Nicolson in the previous general election. Many feel the need for the "grass roots" to have more say.

Those "grass roots" are increasingly impatient of opposition for the sake of opposition, of a party behaving as if it were wholly right and all others wholly wrong. They want to be able to say in which of its policies a party is right or wrong, which of its personalities they admire, whether it should work together with some other party or not, whether they want more women in parliament, or representatives of their own ethnic or religious group, whether they prefer an MP who can be relied upon to toe the party line or one who will vote according to his own convictions.

Proposals to change the British electoral system should take account of all these things, not only of the obvious mis-representation of the parties.

3

Radical Reform

The systems so far considered have been developed to remedy, to a greater or less extent, particular faults seen to exist in the X-vote system commonly used in British parliamentary and other elections. A different approach is the radical one of devising afresh a system designed to serve with certainty the purpose for which an election is held. What is that purpose? Again there are two radically different answers. One assumes the existence of organized political parties and treats these as the units for which fair representation should be secured. The other takes as its unit the individual voter and seeks to give effect to his wishes, whether they have anything to do with a party or not.

PARTY LIST PR

In contrast to the United Kingdom, countries on the continent of Europe have long accorded legal recognition to the organized political parties; hence, when protests were made about unfair election results, it was natural for them to seek a remedy in systems based on voting for a party, not for an individual candidate, seats being awarded to each party in proportion to the votes cast for it.

This is a simple conception but in practice involves complications which give rise to statements such as that there are 300 kinds of proportional representation.

The first difficulty arises in calculating what number of seats is proportional to a party's votes. That seems at first obvious: if a party receives half the votes in the country it should have half the seats in the parliament; if it gets only a tenth of the votes it should have one tenth of the seats. But the voters are never so obliging as to give one party exactly half the votes and another exactly one tenth. What is to be done with the awkward fractions?

Suppose there are five seats to be shared between two parties. If these have respectively three fifths and two fifths of the votes, no difficulty arises. Each complete fifth of the votes gives a party one of the five seats. Now suppose they have respectively 52 and 48 per cent of the votes. Four of the seats can be awarded by the quota of one fifth – two to each party – leaving one seat over. It seems sensible to award this to the party with the more votes left over – 12 rather than 8 – and this gives the fair result of three seats for the larger party and two for the smaller. However, experience with the use of this largest remainder system soon showed that it is not always fair. Suppose the smaller party splits and submits two lists which receive respectively 35 and 13 per cent of the votes. The result will then be:

	votes, %	complete quotas	remainder	total seats
Party A	52	2	12	2
Party B1	35	1	15	2
Party B2	13	0	13	1

Only three seats are decided by the full quota, leaving two to be allotted to the largest remainders, and each of the B parties has a larger remainder than Party A. Hence the latter, although still having its clear majority of 52 per cent of the total votes, wins only two seats instead of three. Such effects have actually occurred, in the Swiss canton of Ticino and in Denmark, and have indeed been produced deliberately. In the Danish election of 1947, the "Liberal Party of the Capital" was formed not to promote any distinctive policy but simply to exploit the possibility of extra seats.

A suggested remedy for this was to allot the remaining seats not to the largest remainders but to the largest parties, but this also was found to be far from satisfactory. An actual result in Ticino was:

Conservatives	614 votes
Radicals	399 votes
	1,013

There being five seats to be filled, the quota was 202, which gave the Conservatives three seats and the Radicals one, with remainders of 8 and 197 respectively. Allocation of the last seat to the larger party gave it four seats to the Radicals' one, while obviously the proportional result would be three to two.

The number of cases in which seats remain to be allocated after division by the full quota can be reduced by using a smaller quota, for instance the Droop quota of (in the election of five people) one more than one sixth of the total valid votes.* This is the smallest number of votes a candidate must have to be sure of election, for six candidates could each get one sixth of the votes but only five could get more. If this is applied to the Ticino example above, the quota will be 169, which goes into 614 three times and into 399 twice, allocating all five seats at once. Use of the Droop quota does not entirely dispose of the problem of remainders, but greatly reduces it.†

Another method of dealing with remainders is to pool them over a larger area. An example of how this is done is given in the official regulations for Belgian elections, which involve two stages. First, in the 20-member city of Antwerp, a quota is found by dividing the 516,948 valid votes by 20, giving 25,847, and this is divided into each party's total votes, seats being awarded according to the whole numbers in the resulting quotients:

	votes	*quotient*	*seats*
Christian Socialists	209,320	8.098	8
Socialists	197,505	7.641	7
Liberals	49,641	1.920	1
Flemish Union	42,799	1.655	1
Communists	11,688	0.452	0

This disposes of 17 seats, leaving three still to be allocated. The other two constituencies in the province of Antwerp, Malines and Turnhout, have respectively four seats allocated and two over; five seats allocated and one over. In all, six seats remain to be allocated. In the second stage, those constituency parties that have declared themselves to be in alliance over the whole province have their remainders pooled (but excluding any party that has not in any constituency either won a seat or polled two thirds of the quota – in this example the Communists). In this second stage the distribution of seats is calculated by a different method – see below. The effect is

* See below, p 48.
† For further discussion of quotas, see *Representation*, nos 78 to 81.

to make the vote much more nearly equal in value for all parties, correcting the initial under-representation of the smaller parties.

	Chr. Soc.	Soc.	Lib.	Flem. U.
seats won in first stage	14	10	1	1
votes per seat	28,254	28,407	71,713	61,012
total seats won	16	11	3	2
votes per seat	24,687	25,825	23,904	30,506

A system that avoids remainders altogether and has now become general was invented by Victor d'Hondt (1882). The procedure is at first perplexing. It consists in taking each party's total of votes, dividing each in turn by 1, 2, 3, etc., as far as may be necessary, and taking the n largest of these quotients to fill n seats. Thus, in the 1979 election to fill Luxembourg's six seats in the European parliament, the result was:

	Christian Socialist	Democrat	Socialist Worker	Social Democrat	Comm.	Liberal	Rev. Comm.
votes	351,942	274,345	211,097	68,310	48,738	5,595	5,027
divided by 2	175,971	137,173	105,549				
divided by 3	117,314	91,448					

Thus, three Christian Socialists were elected, two Democrats and one Socialist Worker. Why? The reason for this apparently odd procedure is that the method aims at making the average number of votes required to elect a member as nearly as possible equal for all parties; in this case it is 117,314; 137,173 and 211,097 respectively. The largest party must obviously have at least one seat. If we gave the same party the second seat, it would have one member per 175,971 votes, while the second and third largest parties would each have no seats for a larger number of votes. Therefore the second seat must go to the Democrats, the third to the Socialist Workers. At this stage it is right to give the Christian Socialists a second seat, since their votes-per-seat average will be higher than that of any other party would be if it received that seat. The same reasoning applies to the allocation of the remaining seats. The nth largest quotient (117,314 in the example) is known as the electoral quotient.

It is this method which is used to fill the extra seats awarded to the parties in the second stage of a Belgian election. In the Antwerp example, the position in the whole province at the end of the first stage is:

	Christian Socialists	Socialists	Liberals	Flemish U.
votes	394,991	284,074	71,716	61,012
seats won	14	10	1	1

Dividing each party's total votes by one more than the number of seats it already has, we find as follows the six largest quotients to fill the six remaining seats:

Christian Socialists	Socialists	Liberals	Flemish U.
26,333	25,825	35,857	30,506
24,682	23,673	23,904	20,337
23,235		17,928	

It will be noticed that the number of votes needed to elect one member increases from the largest party to the smallest; this is generally true under the d'Hondt system. The advantage to the largest party is tiny compared with what usually happens in a British general election (in 1979 the Conservatives elected one MP per 40,406 votes, the Liberals one per 391,373) but some countries have thought it worth while to devise means of reducing it. One motive for this has been a desire to avoid forcing parties into alliances which are not justified by their real similarity. (Compare the splitting of parties to exploit the largest remainder – p 33.) Still taking the Luxembourg example, it will be seen that the four smallest parties have a total of 127,670 votes but no representation; if they had combined as one party they, instead of the Christian Socialists, would have secured the sixth seat. Some countries do indeed allow *apparentement*, i.e. two or more parties may choose to have their votes pooled, and this would appear sensible in the case of the Communists and Revolutionary Communists but probably not for the other two parties.*

In Sweden, a committee set up to consider reducing the handicap on the smaller parties introduced Sainte-Laguë's formula, according to which division is by successive odd numbers instead of by 1, 2, 3,

* For a discussion of alliances under a very different system, see below, p 92.

etc. This, however, was thought to weigh too heavily in the opposite direction and the advantage to small parties was reduced by dividing initially by 1.4 instead of 1. This arrangement was adopted by Sweden in 1952 and also by Norway. Another device, with the object of preventing a proliferation of small parties, is to demand a certain minimum of votes for entitlement to one seat, e.g. in the Federal Republic of Germany to exclude all parties receiving less than 5 per cent of the total votes, in Israel all with under 1 per cent.

CHOOSING FROM THE LISTS

In addition to these mathematical variations, the basic idea of counting votes for a party and awarding seats in proportion to them has been modified for a quite different reason: to give the voters a say in which persons shall be elected to represent the parties.

The party list system is seen at its simplest in Israel, where the whole country is one constituency, each party submits a list of candidates, votes are cast for a party, and each party is awarded, by the d'Hondt rule, seats in proportion to its votes (parties with less than one per cent of the votes being excluded). If a party has enough votes to entitle it to one seat, the candidate who appears first on its list is elected; with twice as many votes the second candidate also will be elected, and so on.

In most countries using such systems, modifications have been introduced to give the voter some degree of power to alter the order of names on the list. No two of these systems are identical, their mechanism can be complex, and the degree of power given to the voter varies from negligible to very great. The same system as in Israel (but using each *département* as a constituency, not the whole country) was applied to the three French elections of 1945 and 1946. Its impersonality was widely disliked, and in the third election a concession was made allowing the voter to express a preference for one candidate within a party list. This, however, was quite valueless, since such a preference became effective only if expressed by more than half of the voters supporting that party. In practice, only a few voters expressed a preference. Some others of these modifications do give really substantial power to the voter. One of the most effective, which is also one of the simplest, is the Belgian.

A Belgian ballot paper is reproduced in figure 10. A party may

Muster eines (französischsprachigen) Stimmzettels*

MODELE II.

(Modèle visé à l'art. 127, alinéa premier.)
(*Moniteur belge* du 28 avril 1929, erratum 5 mai 1950.)

Arrondissement . . . .

Election de . . . . *représentants.*

Election de . . . . *sénateurs.*

Le . . . . 19 . .

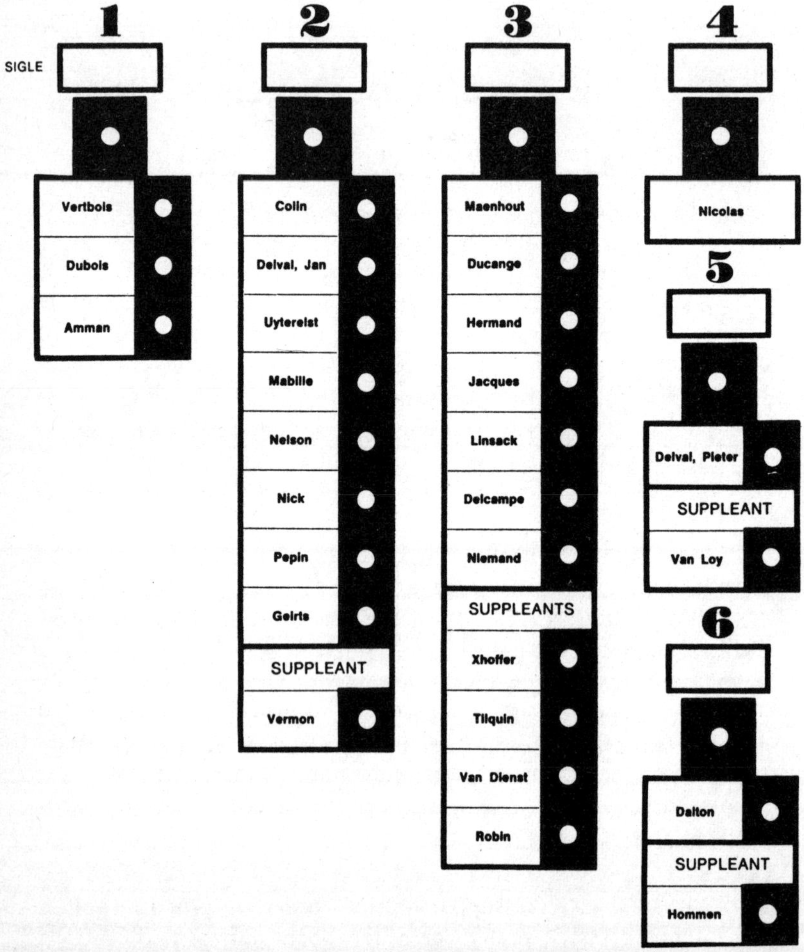

* *From:* A. Delcroix, Recueil des lois électorales belges – Verzameling der belgische kieswetten, Brüssel, 1977, S. 83.

Figure 10 Belgian Ballot Paper

present as many candidates as there are seats to be filled, or fewer, besides *suppléants* to be elected in case of casual vacancies, and there may be a 'list' of a single independent. The voter blacks out either the white spot at the head of a list – indicating that he votes for that party and accepts its candidates in the order the party has placed them – or the white spot beside one candidate's name. This also counts as a vote for the party but operates to change the order of the names. The voter may also indicate a personal preference for one of the *suppléants*. The number of seats a party is to receive having been determined as described on page 35, the candidates to fill these seats are decided as follows:

All the list votes (i.e. those marked at the top of the list) form a pool from which the candidates, in their order on the list, draw in succession as many votes as are necessary to make their personal votes up to the electoral quotient. Suppose that quotient is 3,750, that list 1 includes three candidates, A, B and C in that order, and that the votes for that party are:

list votes	4,000
preferential votes for A	500
preferential votes for B	500
preferential votes for C	3,000
	8,000

Since the party's total votes amount to twice the quotient (and 500 votes over) it will have two seats. Candidate A, having been placed by the party first on the list, has first claim on the 4,000 list votes; he takes 3,250 of these to make his 500 personal votes up to the quotient of 3,750. This leaves 750 list votes still available. Candidate B, being second on the list, has first claim on these, but they are insufficient to bring him up to the quotient, so C takes his turn and is elected.

While a candidate whom a party has placed first on its list is practically certain of election, the voters do have, and do use, very substantial power to override the party's choice for the lower places. Also, personal votes given to the head of the list, though they may appear at first sight pointless, can have their uses. In the 1974 election, the heavy personal vote for Leo Tindemans, the Christian

Socialist leader, must have helped him to be accepted as the head of a coalition government.

A different attempt to introduce a personal element has been made in the Federal Republic of Germany. The Weimar Republic used a rigid party list system as in Israel, whose absence of any personal element was criticized. Germans were under the impression that the British system was a personal one (in fact it is a party list of one name!) and when elections were resumed after the Second World War a mixture of the two systems was introduced. Details of this have been changed from time to time but in its present form the system works as follows. Half the seats in the Bundestag are filled exactly as for the House of Commons. Each party also submits a list of candidates in each Land, and the elector casts a second vote for one of these lists. These second votes are used to correct the distortions produced by the first. Excluding any party that has polled less than 5 per cent of the second votes and has won fewer than three seats by first votes, each party is awarded seats in proportion to its total of list votes over the whole country, these seats being distributed among the Länder according to population. If, for example, in any Land a party has won two seats by first votes but proportionally is entitled to five, it receives three additional members from the top of the list.

The West German system is more personal than the British in one respect. If in his constituency there is one candidate whom the elector finds personally admirable though standing for the 'wrong' party, he can express that admiration without helping that candidate's party – only second votes make any difference to a party's number of seats – and he casts his second vote for the party he favours. In practice, however, there is usually little difference between a candidate's first votes and the second votes for his party in the same constituency. An outstanding exception was Rolf Dahrendorf in the 1969 election; he polled nearly twice as many votes as his party. However, this amounted only to a cheer for him and made no difference to his election. Belonging to the smallest of the three parties, he had no chance of election for a single-member constituency. He was elected, but not because the voters admired him: the FDP had placed him first on its list, thus ensuring his election even if the voters had disliked him.

Also, first votes are an unreliable measure of personal popularity, because they are affected by tactical voting. This was noticeable in the 1980 election, when many voters, encouraged by their party

Stimmzettel

für die Bundestagswahl im Wahlkreis **18 Bergedorf** am 3. Oktober 1976

Sie haben 2 Stimmen

hier 1 Stimme	hier 1 Stimme
für die Wahl	für die Wahl
eines Wahlkreisabgeordneten (Erststimme)	einer Landesliste (Partei) (Zweitstimme)

Erststimme (Wahlkreisabgeordneter):

1	Schmidt, Helmut — Bundeskanzler — Hamburg 62, Neubergerweg 80 — **SPD** — Sozialdemokratische Partei Deutschlands	◯
2	Dr. Reimers, Stephan — Theologe — Hamburg 52, Tönninger Str. 50 — **CDU** — Christlich Demokratische Union Deutschlands	◯
3	Bodeit, Wolfgang — Oberfähnrich a. D. — Hamburg 60, Cesar-Klein-Ring 4 — **F.D.P.** — Freie Demokratische Partei	◯
4	Peemüller, Hans-Heinz — Rentner — Hamburg 72, Meilerstraße 7 — **AUD** — Aktionsgemeinschaft Unabhängiger Deutscher	◯
5	Hetzer, Hans — Schornsteinfeger — Hamburg 26, Horner Weg 47a — **DKP** — Deutsche Kommunistische Partei	◯
10	Prien, Hans — Geschäftsführer — Hamburg 28, Klgv. 114, Parz. 502 — **NPD** — Nationaldemokratische Partei Deutschlands	◯

Zweitstimme (Landesliste / Partei):

◯	**SPD** — Sozialdemokratische Partei Deutschlands — Schmidt, Wehner, Dr. Apel, Glombig, Dr. Meinecke	1
◯	**CDU** — Christlich Demokratische Union Deutschlands — Blumenfeld, Rühe, Dr. Reimers, Damm, Francke	2
◯	**F.D.P.** — Freie Demokratische Partei — Frau Schuchardt, Kirst, Weber, Bodeit, Czerwionka	3
◯	**AUD** — Aktionsgemeinschaft Unabhängiger Deutscher — Frau Johannsen, Paasch, Frau Peemüller, Dr.-Ing. Heydt, Frau Benter	4
◯	**DKP** — Deutsche Kommunistische Partei — Erlebach, Wienecke, Hoff, Frau Luth, Stürmann	5
◯	**EAP** — Europäische Arbeiterpartei — Hellenbroich, Frau Hopf, Frau Tannen, Beimel	6
◯	**GIM** — Gruppe Internationale Marxisten — Hackbusch, Gleiss, Zamory, Lierow	7
◯	**KPD** — Kommunistische Partei Deutschlands — Lenze, Stamer, Wischmann, Heide	8
◯	**KBW** — Kommunistischer Bund Westdeutschland — Plümer, Frau Oberkampf, Denk, Rochlitz, Schween	9
◯	**NPD** — Nationaldemokratische Partei Deutschlands — Sabrautzky, Timmermann, Frau Rahff, Dr. Dr. Ohnesorge, Müller	10

Figure 11 West German Ballot Paper

organizations, were trying to use the system to express approval of the coalition between Social Democrats (SPD) and Free Democrats (FDP). Many FDP voters, knowing that their candidate had no chance of election in a single-seat constituency, sacrificed their opportunity to express approval of him personally, casting their first votes for the SPD candidate and only their second for their own party. As for SPD supporters, there was no way in which they could both maximize their party's representation and help their FDP partners.

During the last few years the West German system, or some variant of it, has received in Britain an amount of attention quite out of proportion to its merits. This has arisen largely from the report, in June 1976, of a committee set up by the Hansard Society for Parliamentary Government. This report lists a number of objections to the present system, but only those relating to the mis-representation of parties. Nowhere is there any mention of the discontents of voters who are "represented" by an MP they personally dislike, or by a right-winger when they would prefer a left-winger of the same party (or vice versa), of the inability of voters to show whether they think Party A should work with Party B or have nothing to do with it, or any other of the failures to reflect adequately the voters' opinions. So why did the committee not recommend a straight-forward party list system? Because it attached great value to the link which the single-member system is supposed to give between an MP and his constituents. (Or perhaps because many MPs are known to believe in this and may more easily be persuaded to accept a reform that preserves some single-member constituencies.) Hence the recommendation of something like the West German system. But the report produces a variant that is worse than the original. It is less efficient even in giving fair representation of parties, for (in order to minimize interference with the existing constituencies) it proposes that only a quarter of the total seats (instead of half as in Germany) should be used for topping up. This must often be inadequate; for instance it would have sufficed to give proportional representation of the main parties in the 1979 election to West-minster, but in the EEC election the same year would have left the Conservatives still substantially over-represented.

Much more serious, it introduces what is really a confidence trick on the electors. To decide which individual candidates should fill the additional seats, it suggests either selection by the parties or, preferably, that

The voter could retain control: candidates could be placed in order according to their performance in the constituency elections. . . . We have decided that the best method would be to use as the determining factor the percentage vote they obtained.

That by this means "the voter could retain control" is frankly nonsense. The voter might be led to believe that he was exercising some control, but anyone with political experience knows that the control would still be exercised, as it is now, by the tiny minority of party activists who choose the candidates for places where the party is strong. That in the last election the Conservative candidate polled 61 per cent in the City of London and Westminster but only 10 per cent in Stepney and Poplar has nothing to do with their respective personal merits in the voters' eyes. The percentage as the determining factor is itself open to question, for it is greatly affected by the number and strength of third and fourth parties. Should Labour's "best loser" in 1979 be the man who polled 49 per cent of the votes in a straight fight in Dudley West, losing by 1,139 votes, or the man who, with 46 per cent in a 4-cornered fight in Preston North, lost by only 29 votes? But those are only minor points. The fatal objection to the "best losers" variant is that it pretends to give the voter some say in selecting the person to occupy a given seat, while in reality doing nothing of the sort. It would even destroy the minimal power which the British voter now has in that respect. Suppose that an MP, in one way or another, has so disappointed the people who voted for him that some, in the next election, refuse to vote or even vote for a different party. If (and only if) he represents a marginal constituency, those personal votes will be enough to turn him out. But under the Hansard committee's scheme he would almost certainly be put back again, contrary to his constituents' wishes. For he would lose only by a small margin and so be among the "best losers".

Simply to tot up over a large area votes cast in single-member constituencies would also destroy one advantage that the Germans have over the British: removal of the obstacle to the nomination of women, members of ethnic minorities or any supposedly unpopular groups.* Far more German than British women find their way into parliament, but most of them are elected by the multi-member Land constituencies; in the other half of the Bundestag their record is no better than the British.

* See below, p 134ff.

Of all party list systems, the Swiss has by far the largest personal element. There is no casting of votes for a party as such. The elector has as many votes as there are seats to be filled, and may distribute these among the candidates as he wishes, with or without regard to party. He may also cumulate two votes on one candidate. Apart from the cumulation, voting is the same as in a London borough council election (p 24) but instead of declaring elected the candidates with the most votes, the returning officer first totals the votes cast for the candidates of each party and awards seats in proportion to those totals. Each party's seats go to the candidates with the highest votes; their position on the ballot paper is immaterial. A similar system is used in Luxembourg.

It will be seen that this enables the voter to do what none of the other list systems permit: to support a cause that cuts across the party lines. Such a cause was the separation of the mainly French-speaking Jura from the mainly German-speaking canton of Bern. Its supporters formed the Rassemblement Jurassien, but this did not operate as a separate party – as under other list systems it would have been obliged to do. It had supporters (and opponents) in all of the established parties and the people who at that time were plastering the canton with 'Jura Libre' posters just gave their votes to autonomist candidates regardless of party. The first election (1976) in the new canton of Jura showed the voters' opinions very clearly: the Rassemblement Jurassien won two thirds of the seats. Its secretary general got the highest poll in the canton (14,397 votes against 6,610 for the next most popular candidate of the same – Socialist – party), its vice president (Christian Democrat) polled nearly twice the votes of the next CD candidate, and the only woman elected was a leading member of the autonomist women's organization.

While the Swiss system does give the voter a much wider and more effective choice between personalities, it is still inferior in this respect to the 'supervote' described in the next section. The preference for one candidate over another (one vote or two) is restricted, and a vote for one candidate may still contribute to the defeat of another candidate whom that voter favours. All party list systems share the defect that a vote given on purely personal grounds counts also for a party and therefore may contribute to the election of a candidate that voter does not want.

"SUPERVOTE": THE SINGLE
TRANSFERABLE VOTE

An entirely different approach to the design of an electoral system takes the voter as its starting point – not the party – and seeks to give effect to the wishes of every voter, whatever they may be and whether they have anything to do with party or not.

Two things are necessary: the voter must be given a free choice among as many candidates as may wish to seek his support, and there must be at least a high probability that the choice he expresses will affect the result of the election in the way the voter wishes.

Elections to the British House of Commons clearly fulfil neither requirement. The voter's choice is extremely limited – to one candidate of each of several parties – so that, for instance, a voter in the 1979 election who wished to keep Labour in office and who lived in Bristol South East had to vote for Tony Benn, while if he had moved to Stevenage he had to vote for Shirley Williams, and even before the party split soon afterwards it was obvious that those two people did not represent the same thing. When the United Kingdom was considering whether to join the European Community, the voters could not, by their votes, influence the decision. Anyone wanting a Conservative government and living in Tunbridge Wells had to vote for a man keen on joining, while one in Banbury had to vote for one equally keen to stay out. Save in those few constituencies where a party's vote is so large that it could be split between two candidates and still leave each with more votes than any other party, it is not possible for any party to offer its supporters a choice between left- and right-wing, pro- and anti-Marketeer, man and woman, white and black. Moreover, even the limited choice that is expressed may not represent the voter's real opinion. It is generally accepted that supporters of a small party often do not vote for its candidate because they fear that their vote will be wasted on someone who has no chance of election and they therefore vote for one of the two largest parties to keep out the other. This applies not only to a party that is small in the country as a whole but to one that is in a hopeless position in a particular constituency. There is evidence that Labour support in Orpington is much larger than its 12 per cent or so of the poll suggests; many who would really prefer a Labour MP vote Liberal as the only hope of ousting the Conservative. Similarly in a place like Rochdale there are likely to be many Conservatives who

vote for the Liberal MP rather than risk having him replaced by a
Labour one. There is need both for a wider choice and for removal
of the obstacles to its honest expression created by the knowledge
that there is a high risk of its having no effect, or even the opposite
effect to that intended.

The solution was worked out in principle by Thomas Wright Hill
in 1821, and was applied by his son, Rowland Hill (the initiator of
the penny post) to the election of a committee by the boys of his
school. Any boy who wished to serve stood out before the class,
and the rest voted by standing beside the boy they most wanted. It
soon dawned upon those in the largest group that not all of them
could really be needed to elect that most popular boy; some were
wasting their voting power there and would be more usefully
employed helping another candidate of whom they approved. At
the other end of the scale, those standing almost alone by a candidate
who clearly had no chance of election transferred themselves to the
most congenial of those still in the running. The process ended with
equal groups round as many boys as had to be elected, with perhaps
a few left over. Nearly every voter found he had contributed to the
election of a representative he wanted.

This is in essence what is now known as the single transferable
vote system of proportional representation. A form of it adaptable
to the secret ballot was put forward by CCG Andrae in Denmark
in 1855, and in Britain by Thomas Hare soon after the 1857 general
election in a pamphlet entitled 'The Machinery of Representation'.
It was elaborated in Hare's treatise on 'The Election of Representatives, Parliamentary and Municipal', published in 1859 and running
into four editions.

A number of modifications have since been introduced, particularly to eliminate all element of chance in the count, but the essential
principle remains unchanged: one person, one vote; election of
several representatives together, each by a quota, not a majority, so
that the votes of electors holding different opinions can all be
effective; transfer of the vote, on the voter's instructions, from a
candidate it cannot help to elect to one it can help. Hare envisaged
that any elector should be able to support any candidate anywhere
in the kingdom, his vote being used first in his own locality but, if
it did not become effective there, being transferable outside it. This
would give the most complete possible utilization of all votes. With
the then electorate of only one million it might not appear too
formidable a task, and with computers it would be perfectly prac-

ticable even with our present electorate of 41 million, but in the meantime the tendency has been to propose, for parliamentary purposes, relatively small constituencies, returning round about five members each.

There is some conflict between the desire to make effective the highest possible number of votes and the desire to have a constituency small enough for the voter to feel at home in it, have personal knowledge of the candidates and not be confronted by an inordinately long ballot paper. However, this conflict is not so serious as may at first appear, for the advantage of adding seats falls off rapidly after the first few. This can be shown by plotting a graph of the number of seats against the number of votes that have no effect on the result ($\frac{\text{total votes}}{\text{seats} + 1}$). There is a huge difference between a single-seat and a 5-seat constituency, very little between a 20- and a 25-seat.

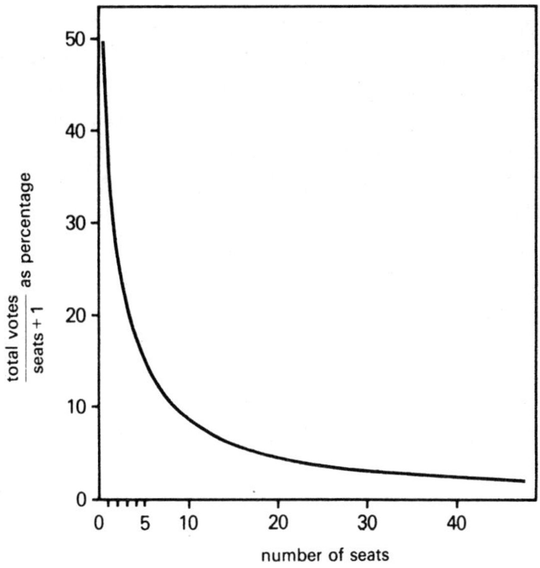

Figure 12

How the single transferable vote works can be explained by taking as an example an actual election in which there were no organized parties but there could be seen various groupings that might be expected to influence a voter's choice. One such example is an election

in 1978 for the Church of England Pensions Board. There were five
places to be filled, and the numbers voting "1" for each of the nine
candidates were:

Archdeacon JM Evans	20
Mr H Gracey	82
Mr CJ Griffiths	7
Mr S Davenport	34
Sqn Ldr PG Driver	90
Mrs V Spencer Ellis	16
Head Deaconess M Parker	20
Mr ERF Pogmore	21
Capt. P Shaw	8
total	298

Are any of these voters in the position of the boys unnecessarily
supporting a candidate who is elected without their help? If so, how
many? To answer these questions we must determine what is the
smallest number of votes that will certainly ensure a candidate's
election. Out of the total 298 votes, six candidates could each get
one sixth of that number (49.6) but only five could each get more;
therefore any candidate with 49.67 votes or more must be one of
the five elected. (Why the decimals? That will appear shortly.) Two
candidates, Driver and Gracey, exceed that total and are declared
elected, and each has a large surplus of votes that are not needed
to elect him. The people who have cast those votes which Driver
does not need must now be asked for whom they wish them to be
used instead.

But *which* of all those 90 people must be asked to choose again?
If they were voting openly like Thomas Hill's boys, we can imagine
that there is a quota of chairs round each candidate and that when
these are full the late-comers go to their next choice. The equivalent
in an election using ballot papers would be for the returning officer
to transfer the last so many papers on top of the elected candidate's
pile. That, however, will immediately be challenged as much too
chancy and what is actually done is in effect to consult *all* of the
elected candidate's supporters as to which of them should move.
That is, the returning officer re-examines all of the elected candidate's
papers and then does simple proportion sums. Suppose Driver had
just twice as many votes as he needs, so that out of every two he
can spare one. So if 20 people, by voting "2" for Davenport, have
asked to have their votes transferred to him, 10 of those votes go

to Davenport, the other 10 staying with Driver for his quota. *Which ten?* In elections to the Irish Dáil it is the top papers in the re-sorted pile, and in an election involving many thousands of votes it is unlikely that the element of chance involved in this has ever affected the result of an election, but when the number of voters is relatively small there is a risk well worth removing. If Davenport were later at the bottom of the poll, those votes he received from Driver would have to be transferred again, and it might then happen, for instance, that those transferred were mainly papers marked "3" for Parker and those left behind "3" for Pogmore. Therefore, always in small elections and increasingly in big ones too, all element of chance is removed by removing the selection of papers for transfer: instead of transferring half of those 1-Driver, 2-Davenport papers, all of them are transferred, the value of each being marked down to one half, or 0.50 – that is where the decimals come in.

Of course in practice the value will not be a convenient fraction like one half. Driver in fact had 90 votes when he needed only 49.67, a surplus of 40.33. Of his 90 supporters, three had marked no second preference. The other 87 papers were used to transfer the 40.33 surplus, so each of them became worth $40.33/87 = 0.46$, with 0.31 left over. It should be noted that each voter has still exercised one vote. Those who were interested only in Driver had it counted wholly for him; those who were willing to transfer their vote to some other candidate gave Driver the 0.54 of a vote that he needed for election, the other 0.46 of the vote going to their second preferences (or third if the second preference was Gracey).

Gracey's surplus is utilized in the same way. We then find – see the result sheet on the next page – that there are three places still to be filled and seven candidates still in the running for them. Griffiths has the smallest number of votes and clearly cannot be elected, so the votes of his supporters (the original 7 plus those he acquired by transfer) are utilized by transferring each to the candidate marked by that voter as his next preference among the six who remain. Since there is no question of having to retain any votes for Griffiths, no change in value arises. These operations are repeated until all five places are filled. It will be noticed that Evans is elected although he has not quite reached the quota. The only possible further operation would be to transfer Parker's surplus of 2.11, and this is unnecessary since even if it all went to Pogmore the latter would still be well behind Evans for the last place. The reason why the final votes for the five elected candidates add up to less than

Table 1

ELECTION RESULT SHEET FOR   Church of England Pensions Board

NUMBER TO BE ELECTED 5   **TOTAL VALID VOTE** 298   **QUOTA** 49·67

CANDIDATES	First Stage	surplus of Driver	Stage 2	surplus of Gracey	Stage 3	exclusion of Griffiths	Stage 4	surplus of Davenport	Stage 5	exclusion of Shaw	Stage 6	exclusion of Sp. Ellis	Stage 7	Stage 8
Archdeacon J. M. EVANS	20	+ 9.66	29.66	+ 4.92	34.58	+ 2.82	37.40		37.40	+ 3.10	40.50	+ 8.89	49.39	elected
Mr H. GRACEY	82		82.00	− 32.33	49.67		49.67		49.67		49.67		49.67	elected
Mr C. J. GRIFFITHS	7	+ 2.30	9.30	+ 3.69	12.99	− 12.99	−		−		−		−	
Mr S. DAVENPORT	34	+ 10.58	44.58	+ 4.92	49.50	+ 2.00	51.50	− 1.83	49.67		49.67		49.67	elected
Sqn. Ldr P. G. DRIVER	90	− 40.33	49.67		49.67		49.67		49.67		49.67		49.67	elected
Mrs V. SPENCER ELLIS	16	+ 3.22	19.22	+ 3.69	22.91	+ 2.23	25.14		25.14	+ 1.69	26.83	− 26.83	−	
Hd Dss. M. PARKER	20	+ 5.98	25.98	+ 4.92	30.90	+ 0.92	31.82	+ 1.00	32.82	+ 9.30	42.12	+ 9.66	51.78	elected
Mr E. R. F. POGMORE	21	+ 3.68	24.68	+ 2.46	27.14	+ 2.94	29.88		29.88	+ 4.92	34.80	+ 6.41	41.21	
Captain P. SHAW	8	+ 4.60	12.60	+ 7.38	19.98	+ 0.82	20.80		20.80	− 20.80	−		−	
Non-distributable remainders of surpluses		+ 0.31	0.31	+ 0.35	0.66		0.66		0.66		0.66		0.66	
Non-transferable						+ 1.46	1.46	+ 0.83	2.29	+ 1.79	4.08	+ 1.87	5.95	
TOTALS	298		298.00		298.00		298.00		298.00		298.00		298.00	

ERS(EA)1a

Electoral Reform Society

Table 1

five times the quota is that 5.95 votes have gone to waste because the voters numbered too few candidates. If they really knew nothing about the remaining candidates, or disliked all of them equally, of course they were right to stop at that point, but it is an insurance against waste of one's vote to go on numbering as long as one has any real preference at all. It should be clear that (contrary to what happens under X-voting) these later preferences can never count *against* the voter's favourite: the vote remains with that favourite so long as it can be of any use to him, and is transferred only if he is either elected with a surplus or hopelessly defeated.

It will be seen that of the 298 votes cast 250.18 or 84 per cent have contributed to the election of a candidate the voter wants – which is a great improvement on the 50 per cent or so usual in X-vote elections. Of the 298 voters, 246 are represented by their first-preference candidate. Moreover, among the remaining 16 per cent of voters, it is probable that most find among the varied five elected one who is to their taste.

The reasons why a voter directs that his vote shall be transferred from his first preference to a particular candidate may be of many different kinds. The largest single section of Driver's papers went to Davenport, probably because they are both experienced and respected Diocesan Secretaries. When Mrs Spencer Ellis was eliminated, her largest parcel went to Deaconess Parker, thus ensuring that those who particularly wanted a woman on the board got one. That Shaw got the largest share of Gracey's surplus is probably because both belong to the evangelical wing of the church. It is natural that the Archdeacon and the Head Deaconess should attract wide support, with the result that Parker overtook the less widely known Pogmore who had been one vote ahead of her on first preferences. None of these groupings were at all exclusive; with one exception, all the candidates still in the running gained something on each transfer.

In an election where party is uppermost in the voters' minds, this system will give proportional representation of the parties, for if a number of people equal to one quota choose to vote 1, 2, 3 ... *n* for the *n* candidates of one party, the transfers will cause those votes to accumulate on the one most favoured candidate of that party and elect him. Twice as many will elect two, and so on. The proportional representation of parties is not a thing directly sought but is a consequence of the voters' decision to vote on party lines. They may diverge from that pattern to a greater or less extent and this also will be reflected in the result. It is a fallacy to assume that the number of seats won by a party must be proportional to the first-preference votes cast for its candidates and that any divergence from this proportionality must mean that there is something wrong with the system. For instance, there might be one candidate who was personally popular with many people who would not support his party (the position of Churchill at the end of the Second World War); any transfer of those people's votes would take them out of that party and tend to increase the representation of some other party.

"Party" may be replaced by some other grouping; for instance, according to the circumstances of the election, people may vote for all the retiring members or all the "new blood", for white candidates or black ones, men or women, and so on. Such choices may overlap with party ones and each can find expression. A voter who wishes to give full support to one party cannot do so without selecting one of its several candidates for his "1" and he will make that selection according to whatever seems to him important – the candidate's personal qualities, whether he is left-wing or righ-wing, and so forth. Since it is the voters' preferences alone that determine which of a party's candidates fill the seats it wins, a party's elected representatives will be, for example, predominantly left-wing or right-wing, according to which opinion predominates among its grass-roots supporters.

If a voter feels strongly about some matter that cuts across the party lines, he can vote 1, 2, 3 ... for all the candidates with whom he agrees on that matter, while putting first among them any who belong to the party he most favours. All those who wish to promote a particular cause can pool their voting strength for that purpose, no matter how much they may disagree on other things.

Another instance of flexibility is that the single transferable vote enables a number of offices to be filled in one election. Suppose that, in the Church of England example given, it had been necessary to elect also a secretary of the Pensions Board, who would then become an ex-officio member of the board, and suppose Gracey was a candidate for that post. If voting were by X's, it would be necessary to hold the election for secretary first, and declare its result, in order for voters to know whether or not he still required votes to win a place on the board. But with preferential voting the two elections can take place at the same time. If Gracey is not elected secretary, he remains as a candidate for the board and the count for this is not affected. If he is elected secretary, his name is removed from the list of candidates for the board and any vote for Gracey is transferred immediately to that voter's next preference. There may indeed be a whole series of offices for which voting may take place at the same time – president, chairman, vice-chairman, treasurer, etc. – with the same candidates involved in any or all of them. All that is necessary is to agree on an order of priority for the various offices.

A similar procedure can be applied to the filling of a casual vacancy – see below, page 102.

It is these varied capabilities of the system that have caused it to be named "supervote", which conveniently distinguishes it from all other systems with their more limited benefits and avoids long-winded expressions such as "the single transferable vote form of proportional representation" or "preferential voting with quota counting".

4

Theory and Practice I: Fair Shares for the Parties

The United Kingdom has had just one thorough official enquiry into electoral systems, by a Royal Commission which was appointed at the end of 1908 and reported in 1910. There have indeed been since then several Speaker's Conferences, but these are of little value. The MPs composing them cannot have the objectivity expected of a Royal Commission, being all subject to party pressures, and – even more serious – they meet in private and publish none of the evidence submitted to them or the discussions upon it. The report of the last such conference consisted simply of a recommendation for no change in the existing system; it is not possible for any other MP, let alone members of the public, to discover on what grounds that recommendation was made or to judge whether they were sound or not.

In 1910 various schemes for making parliaments and other elected bodies a better reflection of the voters' opinions had been discussed for the best part of a century, but actual experience of proportional systems was very limited. Experience of the single transferable vote on a parliamentary scale was confined to one election in Tasmania. Since 1910, the use both of STV and of party list systems has expanded enormously, but no comparable opportunity has been afforded for discussion of how they have worked. In recent years the subject has been debated in parliament in connection with Northern Ireland, devolution in Scotland and Wales, and direct elections to the European parliament, but the main effect has been to show that most MPs and peers are extremely ill-informed.

There is a strong tendency to reckless generalizations – that such and such an electoral system "always" or "never" produces such and such effects. Assertions that a given system will produce stable or unstable government, many or few parties, national unity or civil strife, cannot be valid, for too many other factors are involved. What an examination of various countries' experience can show is whether there is any consistent tendency of any one system to facilitate such and such a development or to hinder it.

SWITZERLAND

A combination of circumstances made Switzerland a pioneer of electoral experiments. Its history impressed upon its people the need for unity to survive as an independent state, but differences in ethnic origin, language and religion made for disunity. A number of distinguished thinkers turned their attention to these problems, and the autonomy of the cantons enabled new systems to be tried out on a small scale.

A system for the election of a constituent assembly for Geneva was put forward by Victor Considérant in 1842 and elaborated by him in 1846; this influenced the *Association Réformiste*, founded in 1865, which was partly responsible for the first step taken to revise the Swiss electoral laws. The demand for this arose from the bitterness of divisions exacerbated by a system giving representation only to the one largest group in any electoral division. In 1847 the predominantly Roman Catholic cantons attempted to secede from the federation, but their revolt was suppressed by the superior strength of the Protestants in the Sonderbund war. Several elections gave rise to disturbances involving loss of life, one of the most serious being in the canton of Ticino in 1889.* That election gave the Conservatives more than twice as many seats as the Liberals, for nearly the same votes (12,783 votes, 77 seats; 12,166 votes, 35 seats). The resulting dissensions were ended by the intervention of the Federal Council, which recommended a proportional system. This was used first for a constituent assembly and the constitution produced by that Assembly established it for all elections in the canton. It did achieve the desired pacifying effect, which led to Ticino's example being followed by other cantons with similar problems, for instance Geneva, where although Protestants and Catholics were nearly equal in numbers the former dominated the council. The system was changed for the 1892 cantonal elections and the effect was graphically demonstrated by the contrast with federal

* For the full story see *La Démocratie Tessinoise et la Représentation Proportionnelle* by Professor JJ Galland, Grenoble, 1909.

elections eleven months later. The cantonal elections passed off calmly and were followed by no disturbances, but in the federal elections (still under a majority system) political antagonism gave rise to rioting.

By 1909, the same proportional system had extended to over half the cantons and was being advocated for federal elections, a constitutional change which required acceptance in a referendum. The first vote taken, in 1900, rejected change by a 3 to 2 majority of the citizens voting and by 11½ cantons to 10½. Ten years later, there was only a bare majority of citizens against change and 10 cantons against 12 in favour. In 1918 the proposal was carried by a two to one popular vote and 19½ cantons to 2½ and the system then introduced has remained in force ever since, without important change.*

It is a flexible system, which does not tie the voter to blanket approval of any one party but gives considerable scope for expression of the voter's opinions also on other matters. A recent important consequence of this has already been mentioned (page 44); the reflection in Bern election results of the extent of popular feeling in favour of a separate canton of Jura.

The first proportional election to the National Council brought a drastic change in the representation of the parties; since then, they have remained very stable, with between 80.0 and 93.4 per cent of the votes and seats going to the four largest parties and the number of smaller parties fluctuating between five and eight.

SEATS IN THE SWISS NATIONAL COUNCIL

	Radicals	Chr. Dem.	Soc. Dem.	People's	Liberal	others	no. of parties
1917	102	42	19	—	12	7	6
1919	58	41	41	31	9	9	9
1979	51	44	51	23	8	23	12

The change from a five-to-four majority of seats for one party to a situation in which no one party ever approaches half the seats has caused no trouble; on the contrary, it seems to be accepted as much more in accordance with the general Swiss attitude that everyone should have his say. The proportional principle is carried into government, the Federal Council (cabinet) having its composition

* See page 44.

carefully balanced to include not only all major parties but also representatives of all the linguistic and religious groups.

There is also much direct democracy including in the smallest cantons meetings of all citizens, and throughout the country there are frequent referendums – on any measure involving a constitutional change and on any other matter if demanded by a sufficient number of electors. Probably because the Swiss are called to the polls so often, turnout tends to be low, but it varies greatly and when any burning issue is involved, is quite high enough to satisfy British standards.

BELGIUM

Similar circumstances led Belgium to become one of the earliest converts to a proportional system. There again is a heterogeneous state, with over half its population living in the area bordering the Netherlands, and speaking Flemish, while rather less than half live nearer France and speak French. The capital, Brussels, is a somewhat uneasy mixture of the two. Before 1899 Belgium used what was then the common European method of the second ballot but not (except in nine cases) in single-member constituencies. Most constituencies returned from two to four members each and Brussels returned eighteen.

The effect of this was to exacerbate the linguistic division by making it appear to coincide with a political one. Flanders elected only Catholics, while French-speaking Wallonia elected only Liberals or Socialists, each having a large minority, unrepresented and increasingly resentful. The country was divided geographically into two solid blocks, differing irreconcilably on whether Belgium should be a secular state and on the privileged position of French in administration, law and education. This state of affairs was found in local as well as in national politics.

A movement for reform, led by Victor d'Hondt, began in 1881 and led to the introduction in 1898 of the present system.* This had three conspicuous effects. First, the Liberal party, which had seemed in danger of extinction, revived to something approaching parity with the Catholics and Socialists. Some smaller parties appeared; many of which have proved ephemeral, but the Flemish and French parties which appeared in the '60's are still flourishing. Second, each of the

---

* For details see pages 34 and 39.

main parties obtained representation in both halves of the country,
ending the appearance of one half being totally opposed politically
to the other. Third, it became usual for members of parliament to
represent their own home territory. Under the old system, for
example, it was impossible for a Flemish Socialist to find a seat in
Flanders; he had to go to Brussels or an industrial town in Wallonia.
But as soon as the Socialist minority in Flanders could get its share
of the seats he returned to represent his own home. There is still
much dissention, but at least the breaking up of Belgium into separate
Flemish and Walloon states appears less likely than it would have
been if the former electoral system had been retained.

In the table below, under "number of parties", the Flemish and
French organizations of the Catholics, Socialists and Liberals
respectively have been counted as separate parties but the number
of seats refers to the two taken together.

SEATS IN THE BELGIAN HOUSE OF REPRESENTATIVES

	Catholic	Socialist	Liberal	Flemish	French	others	no. of parties
1898	112	27	13	—	—	—	4
1900	86	31	34	—	—	1	5
1978	82	58	36	14	11	11	10
1981	61	61	52	20	8	10	12

It is very rare for one party to win the support of more than half
the voters, and nearly all governments are coalitions. Agreement on
these is not always easy, and changes of government are fairly
frequent – but many of these amount to no more than the cabinet
reshuffles which are taken for granted in Britain.

The election of November 1981 was notable for heavy losses by
the hitherto dominant Christian Democrats, large gains by the
Liberals and the appearance of four Ecologist members. The electors
appeared to be in a mood for change. The inconclusive result in terms
of party representation led to six weeks of negotiation, ending in
the formation of a Christian Democrat–Liberal coalition. This
solution was of course arrived at by the party leaders. Would the
position of Belgium be improved if her voters were able to express
directly their views on which combination of parties would be most
acceptable? This (and the effect on the number of parties) will be
discussed further in the next chapter.

THE NETHERLANDS

Belgium's neighbour, the Netherlands, has a rather similar electoral history, but its divisions are overtly religious. Some superficial critics of proportional representation cite the Netherlands as a country where, they say, it has brought a multiplicity of parties and coalition governments that are formed with difficulty and break up with ease. This cannot be true, for the same difficulties existed to an equal or even greater extent before the First World War, when the parliament was elected by the second ballot in single-member constituencies. The many parties, largely based on religious sects ranging from Catholic to Calvinist, go right back to the constitution of 1848; their antagonisms made effective government difficult and twice there was resort to a non-party ministry drawn from outside parliament. The discontent of the unrepresented led first to extensions of the franchise and then, in 1917, to the introduction of a proportional electoral system.

In this, the elector votes for a party list and seats are awarded to each party, by the d'Hondt rule, in proportion to its national total of votes. However, voting is in eighteen separate districts and a party need not submit the same list in each (it will probably put first a candidate known to be popular in that district). The voter is also obliged to cast a second vote for an individual candidate within his party's list. It is these second votes which mainly decide which individuals are elected. A party's votes divided by its seats gives its "list quota" and any candidate whose personal votes reach this number is elected. Any surplus votes he has are transferred to whichever of the as yet unelected candidates the party has placed highest on its list – but omitting any whose personal votes are less than half the list quota.

The new electoral system brought no startling change in the complexion of the parliament, but there have been gradual changes over the years, with the disappearance or merging of some old parties and the rise of new ones. Recently there has been a tendency to less emphasis on religious divisions and a rise in parties of social reform, notably D (for Democracy) '66 and DS'70. The number of parties represented rose initially from 10 to 15 but in the next election dropped again to 10 and has since varied between 7 and 14.

SEATS IN THE DUTCH SECOND CHAMBER

	Catholic	Anti-Revoln.	Christian Historical	Liberal	Social Dem.	D'66	others	no. of parties
1913	24	11	9	32	15	—	11	10
1918	30	13	7	10	22	—	19	15
	Christian Democratic Appeal				Labour			
1977	49			28	53	8	12	11

Voting was compulsory (as in Belgium) until 1970. Removal of this compulsion has hardly affected the turnout, which in 1977 was 87.5 per cent.

LUXEMBOURG

The third Benelux country, Luxembourg, adopted in 1919 a system which has one feature in common with the Swiss: the voter can support a cause that cuts across the party lines. The ballot paper is similar to the Belgian except that each candidate has two squares beside his name, not one. The voter may mark a square at the top of a party list, in which case he gives one vote to each candidate on that list. Alternatively, he exercises a number of personal votes, up to the number of seats to be filled, giving either one or two of these to individual candidates and not necessarily confining himself to a single party. Each party is allotted seats by the d'Hondt rule in proportion to its total of list votes and personal votes for candidates on its list, and these seats go to the candidates with the highest personal votes.

The change from the previous second ballot system was part of a package of reforms including enfranchisement of women and abolition of a property qualification, and arose from a general ferment at the end of the First World War. It did coincide with the end of the previous two-party situation, but was less a cause of this than a response to the demand for representation by the more radical elements whose frustration would have become dangerous if the old system had been continued. The parliament elected in 1979 contains three major parties and four others with only one or two seats apiece.

FINLAND

Finland's use of a proportional system goes right back to 1906, when the country was still a grand duchy within the Russian empire, exercising home rule through a Diet composed of four houses (Nobility, Clergy, Burghers, Peasantry). Following a *coup d'état* in 1899, the country continued in a turbulent state and radical reconstruction was clearly needed. To this end the constitution of 1906 was drawn up, which is remarkable for the original and democratic nature of its provisions. These included universal suffrage (yes, including women) at the age of twenty-four and a single-chamber legislature. The proportional electoral system was essential to the acceptance of this proposal, for, as a contemporary Finnish pamphlet points out*, those four estates of the realm would certainly not have surrendered their powers and privileges if they had not been assured that each of them would have a fair deal and that there would be no possibility that the assembly might be dominated by an extremist minority. An important factor behind their acceptance was the check placed on the power of the assembly by a provision that certain important bills could not become law until after the next general election. This was similar in intention to the power of delay possessed by the British House of Lords, but more effective because Finland's electoral system gives the voter much greater power to express his opinion about a particular measure.

The original 1906 system required the voter to select from a number of different combinations of candidates, but this has since been simplified. The candidates are listed in parties and each is given a number; the ballot paper bears only a circle, in which the voter is required to write the number of one candidate. Each party is allotted, by the d'Hondt rule, seats in proportion to the number of ballot papers on which the voter has placed the identification number of one of its candidates, and which candidates fill those seats is determined by the number of personal votes they receive.

Finland does indeed have a fairly large number of parties represented (eight in the parliament elected in 1979, though only four of these share 85 per cent of the seats), all governments are coalitions and their composition changes fairly frequently. However, it cannot be said that this adds up to instability. Governments that maintain

---

* *The Finnish Reform Bill of 1906*, Helsinki, 1906.

the independence of a tiny democracy in the shadow of its huge totalitarian neighbour are not weak. Government strength rests on the knowledge that it has majority support (64 per cent of the voters in the case of the present government – compared with 44 per cent in the United Kingdom) and government by consent is promoted by the extensive use of all-party parliamentary committees which discuss important questions before they reach the stage of being made the subject of a bill.

SWEDEN

The next Scandinavian state to go proportional was Sweden, in 1907 after an agitation beginning in 1856. The system then in use was the same as the present British X-vote, except that Stockholm was one 22-member constituency, which of course added greatly to the distortion of the result. Agitation for a change began as early as 1856 but succeeded only in 1907, with a law establishing both manhood suffrage and a proportional system based on voting for a party list. The country is divided into 28 constituencies, each electing from 2 to 33 members according to population. The elector votes for a party list and seats are awarded by the odd number Sainte Laguë rule, ie dividing successively by 1, 3, 5, etc. As compared with the d'Hondt rule, this gives an advantage to small parties. The voter has no effective power to alter the order in which his party has placed its candidates. He may indeed cross out names and/or write in others, but to have any effect this must be done by a number of voters far larger than is ever likely to be reached. However, there is an element of personal choice, because if, for instance, a section of a party dislikes the candidate that party has put first on its list and wants to substitute another, it can submit a separate list, headed by its preferred candidate, and ask to have the two lists treated as one party for allocation of seats (*apparentement*). This is very often done. A total of 310 seats are allocated in the 28 constituencies. In addition there are 39 seats (in 1976 this number was reduced from 40, in order to give an odd number of total seats and thus prevent deadlocks*) used to remedy the distortions arising from the existence of some very small constituencies. For this purpose the whole country is treated as one constituency for working out the total seats each party

---

* Compare Tasmania, p 81.

should have and a party with less than that number receives an extra seat (or possibly more than one) in those constituencies where it has the largest remainder of unused votes. Parties with less than 4 per cent of the votes are excluded. The accuracy of party representation is very high; indeed it is pointed out that when the 1979 election resulted in a difference of only some 8,000 votes (out of a total $5\frac{1}{2}$ million) between the two main blocks, the system ensured that it was the larger block which had a parliamentary majority of one seat.

The three parties existing in 1907 have been joined by the Centre (formerly Agrarian) party on the right and the Communists on the left; in few elections has any sixth or seventh party won any seats. The Social Democrats have long been the largest party, sometimes achieving a clear majority and for many years governing either alone or in coalition.

DENMARK

Although Denmark's first proportional election to its lower house of parliament did not come until 1920, it was well ahead of all other European states in electoral experiments. As already mentioned,* it was a Dane, Carl Andrae, who first put forward the single transferable vote form of PR, and this was used in 1856 for the election of 55 out of the 80 members of the single-chamber Rigsraad. In 1866, under a new constitution which established a second chamber (abolished again in 1953), this system was retained for the indirect election of the Landsting (upper house) by electoral colleges which after 1915 were chosen by a party list form of proportional representation. Election by small electoral colleges composed of disciplined party representatives did not give much scope for the advantages of the single transferable vote to show themselves.

Apart from this, the lower house (Folketing) was until 1915 elected by the first past the post system still used in Britain. For many years it was composed of Conservatives and Liberals, but with the extension of the franchise, Radical and Social Democrat parties developed. No one party could obtain a working majority, and uneasy alliances developed between the two older parties on the one side and the two newer ones on the other. In an attempt to eliminate unrest caused by these alliances and to give fairer representation

* p 46.

to the Left, there was introduced in 1915 (operating in the 1918 election) an element of proportional representation. This established party list PR in the capital, but elsewhere a system on the lines of that now used in West Germany – 92 seats filled as before in single-member constituencies and 23 added to reduce the distortion. Public outcry against the inadequacy of this caused it to be replaced before the next election by a proportional system which, with some modifications, has remained in force ever since.

Denmark is divided into 17 constituencies, each divided into as many districts as there are members to elect (two to ten). Each party submits a list of candidates, with the candidate nominated for that district placed first. The voter marks either one party or one candidate and a total of 135 seats are allocated in proportion. An additional 40 seats serve to make the result more accurately proportional. To decide which candidates fill the seats, each candidate is credited with his own personal votes plus his party's votes in the district where he appears first on its list. A party may modify this, either (1) by making its candidates' election depend only on their personal votes, not on their position on the ballot paper, or (2) on the contrary by placing all its candidates in order, not just the first. In this case, any personal votes a candidate has above the number he needs for election are transferred to the candidate the party has placed next in order. Votes are similarly transferred from the candidate(s) with the fewest votes.

The number of parties has increased but the original four continue to share about three quarters of the seats. The total number of parties represented has varied between five and ten.

SEATS IN THE DANISH FOLKETING

	Conservative	Liberal	Radical	Soc. Dem.	others	no. of parties
1913	7	44	31	32	0	4
1918	22	46	31	39	2	5
1979	22	22	10	68	53	10

Although no single party ever holds more than half the seats, there is often a single-party government, that party so adjusting its actions as always to command sufficient support from among the others. Otherwise there is a coalition. The general result is great stability of policy, each government, of whatever composition, maintaining those policies on which there is widespread agreement.

Folketingsvalget 1977

A. Socialdemokratiet

Svend Auken
Per Blendstrup
Henry Grünbaum
Karl Hjortnæs
Søren B. Jørgensen
Jens Kampmann
Kurt Francis Madsen
Alfred Mogensen
Otto Mørch
Marinus Sørensen

B. Det radikale Venstre

Sven Skovmand
Harald Westergård Andersen
Erik Bach
Bernhard Baunsgaard
Henrik Larsen
Grete Lautrup-Larsen
Ketty (Vendelbo) Mikkelsen
Keld Nielsen
Arne Trosborg
Frank Wammen

C. Det konservative Folkeparti

Ellen (Strange) Petersen
Per Bendix
Lene Gammelgaard
Ole Bernt Henriksen
Elisabeth Krog
Oluf Lowzow

E. Danmarks Retsforbund

Erik Arnkil Jørgensen
Preben Faust Anderson
Ib Christensen
Peter de la Cour
Yrsa Nymand
Preben Pedersen
Margit Rønnow
Jesper Schneidelbach
Ib Steckhahn

F. Socialistisk Folkeparti

Ebba Strange
Aage Frandsen
Horst Horster
Hanne Thygesen
Mogens Engsig-Karup
Elmar Jessen
Ove Andersen
Marianne Bentsen-Pedersen
Henning Sørensen
Torben Maintz Andersen

K. Danmarks kommunistiske Parti

Bernard Jeune
Freddy Madsen
Bent Gammelgaard
Ove Peitersen
Bjørn Grøn
Gurli Madsen
Hans Nielsen
Flemming K. Jensen
Knud Erik Kristensen
Jens Asger Hansen

M. Centrum-Demokraterne

Arne Melchior
Christian Arnfast
Metha (Sommer) Christensen
Erik Ib-Larsen
Chr. Møller Kristensen

P. Pensionistpartiet

Frede Jespersen
Johs Andersen
Martin Aubel
H Rossov Jakobsen
Tage Jakobsen
Børge Jensen
Inga Pedersen
Poul Rimmen
Otto Schjerlund

Q. Kristeligt Folkeparti

Inger Stilling Pedersen
Karl Dahl
Kresten Futtrup
Johannes Strunge Nielsen
Arne Rod
Ole Søndergård
Svend Vig

V. Venstre, Danmarks liberale Parti

Ove S. Torp
Anders Andersen
E. Toftegaard Andersen
Uffe Ellemann-Jensen
Knud Enggaard
Bertil Toft Hansen
Ivar Lykke Kristensen
I. C. Mortensen
Anne Cathrine Nygaard
Anna Dorith Skriver

Y. Venstresocialisterne

Steen Folke
Niels Holstein-Rathlou
Ivan Jensen
Viggo Jonasen
Anette Krab-Johansen
Hans Lassen
Jørgen Lenger
Carl Ancher Pedersen
Flemming Ravn Rasmussen
Litha Christiansen
Hans Erik Madsen
Astrid Pedersen
Tine Danckerfjord
Anders Hessel
Karsten Juul-Olsen

Z. Fremskridtspartiet

K. J. Rosleff
John Arentoft
Poul Bjerregaard
Leif Christensen
Chr. V. Gede
Allan Graugaard-Jensen
Børge Halvgaard
Tove Jensen
Ejnar Surrow

Uden for partierne

Tommy Nielsen

Figure 13 Part of a Danish Ballot Paper

NORWAY

Norway has undergone many changes, developing both the franchise and the system of voting, the latter being changed in 1921 from the second ballot in single-member constituencies to proportional representation of parties. There are 19 constituencies, each corresponding to a county (or the capital), electing a total of 155 members. There have been several variations in detail from time to time, of which perhaps the most important was a change in 1953 from the d'Hondt rule to modification of the Sainte Laguë formula, dividing successively by 1.4, 3, 5, 7, etc.; the object of this was to check over-representation of the largest party while not giving undue advantage to small parties. There is still some under-representation of the latter, due to the small number of members elected from some constituencies. A suggestion for adding seats on a national basis has not so far been accepted. The voter has no choice between candidates (though in local government elections he has). The bulk of the seats have continued to be shared by three or four parties, with up to four small ones also represented. Power has shifted towards the Socialists, who have been the largest single party since 1927 and four times have achieved a clear majority. They were in government, first as part of a coalition and then alone, continuously for twenty years from 1945. As in the other Scandinavian countries, there is a large element of government by consent, even with a single-party government, and little drastic change of policy. The result of the latest (1977) election was:

	votes, %	seats	%
Socialists	42.4	76	49.0
Conservatives	24.7	41	26.5
Christian People's Party	12.1	22	14.2
Centre Party	8.6	12	7.7
Socialist Left	4.1	2	1.3
Liberal Party	3.2	2	1.3
others	4.9	0	0

SPAIN

In the period leading up to the Civil War, Spain was using the limited vote. Constituencies returned from 2 to 18 members each and the number of votes that could be used ranged from 1 in the smallest constituency to 14 in the largest. Under the new regime the limited vote is still used for the 207 elected members of the 248-seat Senate, in constituencies mostly electing four members each. With the return to democracy after the death of Franco, a party list proportional system was instituted for election of the Congress of Deputies, each province being one constituency with from 3 to 33 members. Seats are allotted by the d'Hondt rule to parties polling not less than 3 per cent of the votes; the voter has no choice between candidates.

As might be expected in the first free election for many years, a very large number of parties registered (over a hundred), but most of them won no seats and four only one each. A number of centre parties fought as a coalition and after the election combined into a single party. Two socialist parties similarly combined. Because of the large number of parties and the intentional weighting of the system against the small parties, the Union of the Democratic Centre (UCD), with a little over one third of the votes, secured 165 of the 350 seats (47 per cent), the Socialist Workers and their Catalonian Socialist allies coming second with 28.5 per cent of the votes and 118 seats (34 per cent); a purely UCD government was formed.

An important feature of the result is that the UCD is well represented in all provinces. Had a majority system of election been used, the purely local parties of the Basque country and of Catalonia might well have monopolized the representation of their respective provinces, thus dangerously exaggerating their difference from the rest of the country.

GERMANY

The Federal Republic of Germany is in a curious position. Under a proportional system, it is often held up as a model of stability and prosperity, yet a somewhat different proportional system is often blamed for the rise of Hitler and the collapse of the Weimar Republic, and those who take this latter view use it as a blanket condemnation of PR, not only of the Weimar system as contrasted with the present one. A closer look at history is clearly needed.

It is said that the Weimar system produced a large number of squabbling little parties, among which no stable government could be formed. That charge is plausible, for the system was one that offered the maximum encouragement to a growth in the number of parties – votes were counted over the entire country and any party received one seat for every 60,000 votes it polled. These seats went to the candidates the party had placed first on its list. But was this the reason why nine elections under that system gave seats to between 10 and 15 parties? Hardly, for the last pre-first war Reichstag, elected by the second ballot from single-member constituencies, contained 16 parties, not counting five local parties that disappeared automatically with Germany's loss of Alsace-Lorraine and other territories. Nor can the reduction to only three parties in every Bundestag since 1961 be due simply to the clause in the present law which excludes any party polling less than 5 per cent of the second votes, for if that same clause had been applied to the Weimar elections it would have left in every case five, six or seven parties represented. There must have been other influences favouring fragmentation.

Could the Nazi party have triumphed if the system had not allowed it representation while it was still tiny? I was working in Germany in 1929, and according to all my observations the state of the country was such that electors were ready to follow any party that promised them a place in the sun; whether it already had a handful of seats or not was irrelevant. Its percentage vote shot up from 2.4 to 18.5 in the next election, making it easily the second largest party – a position under which, if the British electoral system had been in use, it might have been grossly over-represented. It never attained more than half the seats – 288 out of 647 in the last free election, 1933. Goering said at his trial that under the British system that election would have given the Nazis every seat in the country, and he cannot have been far wrong.

The much greater success of present-day West Germany owes much less to any change in the electoral system than to both its people and their conquerors having learned some lessons. There is neither the bitterness against outside enemies felt to be imposing unreasonable terms nor the "stab in the back" myth that Germany was defeated by traitors in her midst and not in fair fight; the inclination is much more to live down a terrible past. Unfortunately, German prosperity is being used by some people in Britain as an argument for importing their electoral system (on the same grounds, why not the Swiss?), overlooking its inadequacies.

Instead of introducing a really personal choice between candidates within each party, the framers of the post-war German system relied on the allegedly personal nature of the British system (see p 40).

Half the seats in the Bundestag are filled exactly like those in the House of Commons; the other half are allocated to the parties so as to make their total representation as nearly proportional as possible. Originally, these additional seats were allotted on the basis of the votes cast in the single-member constituencies. From 1953 onwards, the German voter has cast two votes – the first for an individual candidate in his single-member constituency, the second for a party list in his province. This does make the system a little more personal than the British, for if there is in the constituency a candidate whom the voter admires personally though disliking his party, the voter can express that admiration by means of his first vote without helping that candidate's party: he gives his second vote to the party he favours and it is these second votes alone which affect the number of seats the party wins. However, as already mentioned (page 40) the practical effect of this is not great.

The Bundestag has consistently been made up of three parties, the nearly equal Social Democrats and Christian Democrats with the much smaller Free Democrats. The election of October 1980 gave this result:

	CDU/CSU	SPD	FDP	"Greens"	others
votes, %	44.5	42.9	10.6	1.5	0.5
seats	226	218	53	0	0

The fourth (ecology) party has never yet won a seat in the Bundestag, though it has done so in some provincial elections. (For a discussion of its position see below, p 70.) All governments have been coalitions, nearly always including the FDP. Some contend that FDP influence is therefore excessive, but no evidence is produced that it does anything other than modify the policy of its coalition partner in a direction acceptable to the majority of the nation. Certainly there is no instability, and in every election extremist parties have fared very badly.

In the 1980 election, Chancellor Helmut Schmidt made it clear that he did not want his Social Democrat party to win a clear majority (nor of course the opposing Christian Democrats); he valued the Free Democrat members as an insurance against pressure by extremists within his own party. In the absence of any choice for the voters between moderates and extremists within any party, this party balance has worked well to produce the kind of government which the majority of the nation appears to desire. However, it would

break down if in any election the Free Demócrats failed to maintain
their rather precarious hold on the 5 per cent minimum vote. Future
stability would be more certain if the electors were able directly to
put their voting strength behind candidates committed to the policies
that most of them favour.

There are, however, signs that many electors would like a choice
not limited to one or other of three parties. In the May 1981 election
to the West Berlin house of representatives, an "alternative list" was
presented by a loose alliance of ecologists, pacifists, civic action
groups, etc., few, if any, of which stood any chance of representation singly but who as an alliance polled 7.2 per cent of the votes
and won 9 of the 133 seats. It will be interesting to see whether
this proves to be a step towards a more flexible system.

AUSTRIA

Any rash assertion that proportional representation "always"
produces many parties and coalitions is disproved by Austria, which
has neither. It is true that the particular system used (basically the
same since the Republic came into being in 1918) does impose a
handicap on small parties but this is tiny compared with the effects
of a system like the British. The result of the latest (1979) election
could hardly have been more proportional, only the Communists
being deprived of their one seat.

		votes, %	seats	%
Socialist party	SPÖ	51.06	95	51.9
People's party	ÖVP	41.9	77	42.1
Freedom party	FPÖ	6.1	11	6.0
Communist party	KPÖ	1.0	0	0

The count takes place in two stages. The votes cast in each of the
nine provinces are divided by the province's number of seats (proportional to its population) and this quotient divided into each
party's votes gives the number of seats that party wins. Those seats
go to the candidates heading the party's list. There will be in each
case a remainder of votes and a remainder of the total 183 seats
not thus allocated. These remainders are pooled over each of two
regions, and the seats not already filled are divided, using the

d'Hondt rule, among those parties that have won at least one seat in the first stage.

The *Documentation* published by the Federal Press Service on 6 May 1979 gives this opinion on Austrian elections since the last war:

> The first election took place in November 1945, under four-power occupation and in conditions of post-war chaos, and ended with a world sensation – 161 of the 165 seats went to the ÖVP and the SPÖ, the Communists obtained four seats. ... The Occupation Powers had refrained from any attempt whatever to intervene or to influence the outcome, the elections had been really free. ... Without 25 November 1945 it is likely that today's Austria would not have been possible ... that the roots of the State Treaty [1955, re-establishing Austria's independence] go back to that day.

The first government was a grand coalition of all three parties. The one Communist minister withdrew after two years; the two big parties continued in coalition until 1966. The overriding need for unity in dealings with the occupation powers having then ended, and the ÖVP having won an absolute majority, this party formed a government alone. In 1970, the SPÖ became the largest party, first forming a minority government and then winning an absolute majority – retained in 1979 for the third successive election. The same prime minister, Dr Bruno Kreisky, has now been in office continuously for nearly twelve years.

ITALY

Italy is the country at present most often chosen by people seeking an example of bad effects resulting from proportional representation. They blame PR either for bringing Mussolini to power or for present instability. To what extent are they justified?

From its foundation as a single independent state in 1871 until 1919, Italy's parliament was elected by a majority system – for nearly all that period the second ballot in single-member constituencies. This failed to advance the young state far along the road to political maturity. Parties were largely mere personal factions and Italy was ruled by "coalition governments with weak and inconsistent pro-

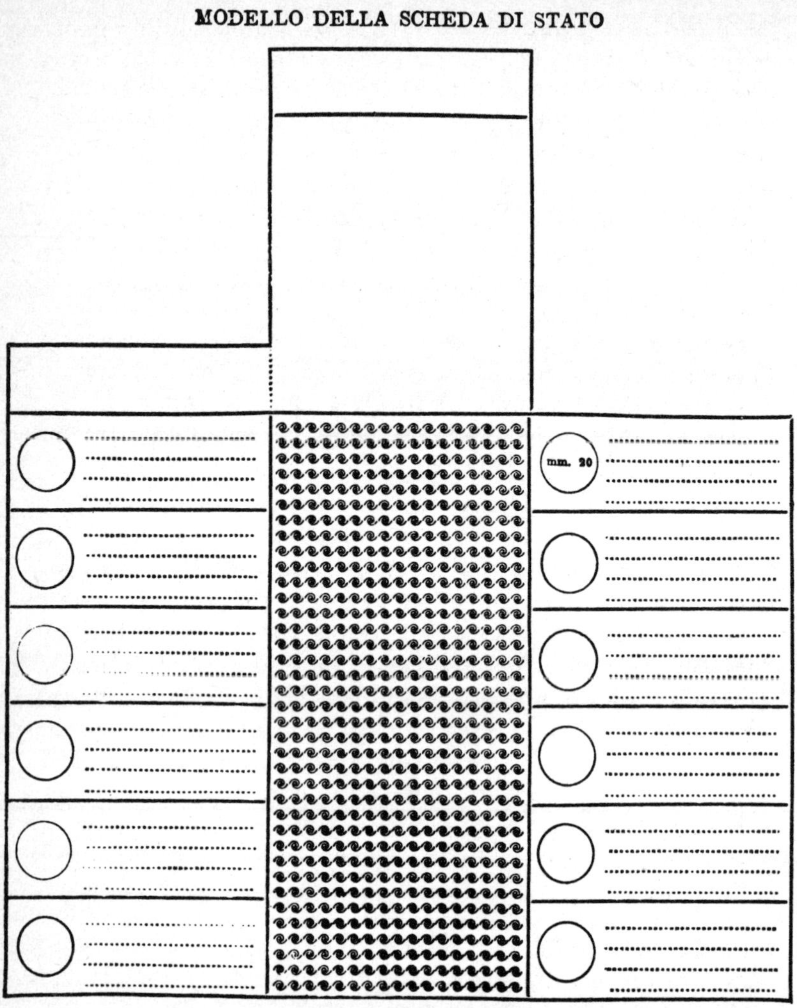

MODELLO DELLA SCHEDA DI STATO

Figure 14 Italian Ballot Paper

grammes propped by the bought support of groups".* A Deputy
tended to be elected for his local influence rather than his political
opinions and, having no fixed political allegiance, to barter his vote
with the administration. In 1919 a proportional system was introduced with general agreement, a motive for this being to promote

* Bolton King and Thomas Okey, *Italy Today*, Nisbet, 1901, p 20.

the formation of parties that were real political groups, with national programmes, instead of personal factions. The system chosen was one of party lists but with some personal choice; in its present form the elector must vote for a party and may in addition record personal votes for up to 3 candidates on that same list if there are 15 or fewer seats to be filled in the constituency, for 4 if there are more than 15. Candidates are elected in the order of their personal votes. Voters who have not used their personal votes (in practice the majority) are deemed to have given them to the first 3 (or 4) candidates on the party's list.

Each of the circles contains the chosen symbol of a party (e.g. the Communist hammer and sickle) and its initials. The voter must strike out the symbol of the party for which he votes and, on the dotted lines beside that symbol, may write in the names of his preferred candidates within that party.

This did produce well organized national parties but did nothing to induce them to co-operate for the common good when co-operation was needed. The Socialists refused to collaborate in government and promoted (with the use of force) industrial unrest which the government did little to check. This, with other factors, inspired the rise of nationalist groups which in their turn resorted to violence. Too many Italians, unfortunately, had yet to learn the lesson that

> in a self-governing people, all parties are responsible for the maintenance of government; ... a party that refuses all share of responsibility for the maintenance of government may render a great disservice to the country. For parliamentary government implies government as well as loyalty to parliament. Parties who refuse to assist in permitting the wishes of the majority to have effect, are in revolt against parliamentary government itself; in the resulting chaos parliamentary government may disappear.*

These nationalist groups included Mussolini's Fascists, who secured 45 seats in the 1921 election and in 1922 formed a government in coalition with 3 other parties. That government changed the electoral law so as to give the party with the most votes two thirds of the seats (other parties sharing the remaining one third proportionally) but in fact the Fascists won the next election without this aid, polling nearly two thirds of the votes. Had a single-member system still been

* John H Humphreys, *Representation*, August 1923, pp 19, 20.

in force, this vote would certainly have given them even more seats. The Italian historian Gaetano Salvemini does not consider that proportional representation was at all to blame for the rise of Fascism; on the contrary it prevented even worse disunity. In the 1919 election,

> under the single-member system, many other seats in northern and central Italy would have fallen to the Socialists. The other groups would have survived mainly in southern Italy. Proportional representation prevented this development. ... It lessened the bitterness of the electoral contest. Under the single-member system the electorate is forced in every constituency to divide itself among no more than two factions, one of which must put the other out of commission. Proportional representation permits each party to show its own electoral strength without being entirely cast aside if in a minority. Each party thinks more of increasing its own votes than of destroying those of its opponents.[*]

With the restoration of democracy after 1945, the difficulties of forming a stable government have continued but are no worse than they were under the old majority system. There has not been a multiplication of parties; the number winning representation was already ten (at a conservative estimate) in 1913 and has remained about the same.

ITALIAN CHAMBER OF DEPUTIES, GENERAL ELECTION JUNE 1979

	votes, %	seats won
Christian Democrat	38.3	262
Communist	30.4	201
Socialist	9.8	62
Neo-Fascist	5.3	30
Social Democrat	3.8	20
Radical	3.4	18
Republican	3.0	16
Liberal	1.9	9
Proletarian	1.4	6
South Tirol	0.6	4
Val d'Aosta parties	0.1	1
Trieste parties	0.2	1
others	1.8	0
	100.0	630

[*] Gaetano Salvemini, *The Origins of Fascism in Italy*, 1942; Torchbooks reprint, 1973, pp 232, 233.

The existence of the large Communist party is a major factor in the continuing difficulty of forming and maintaining a government, and its withdrawal from a five-party coalition occasioned the 1979 election. The then prime minister failed to form a new government and was succeeded by another Christian Democrat who was defeated on economic policy after only five months; his successor was brought down by a scandal involving a masonic lodge. A new development following this may be the beginning of a change in Italian politics. After 35 years of Christian Democrat prime ministers, the post went to a member of the small Republican party, Giovanni Spadolini, who formed a cabinet composed of Christian Democrats, Socialists, Social Democrats and one Liberal. He seems to be in tune with popular demand for firm government to deal with corruption and other evils, and enjoys a high reputation as a journalist and historian, but he would have a better chance of success if the electoral system gave the voters more control over the parties and the warring factions within them and allowed a direct expression of the people's views on what policies should be pursued and which parties should combine for the purpose.

GREECE

Like Italy, Greece as a single state is relatively young and its people have the reputation of being every man his own party. Geographical factors have militated against unification and impeded the growth of great national parties. There have been six new or revised constitutions (1863, 1911, 1926, 1935, 1968 and 1975), many changes of electoral system and five *coups d'état*, three of these occurring while majority systems of election were in use, two under proportional systems. No form of proportional representation was used until 1926; since then most elections have been basically proportional, usually with some weighting in favour of the largest parties. Under both systems there have been frequent changes of government; both have produced sometimes a clear majority for one party, sometimes a coalition. One of the inflated majorities produced by a majority system in 1920 proved harmful: that government led Greece into a disastrous war which was denounced both by Greece's allies and by the opposition – which might have been able to stop that adventure if it had had its rightful share of nearly half the seats.

On the other hand, the absence of a parliamentary majority for one party has not always meant weak government; the coalition government following the 1926 election instituted reforms which probably no one party could have carried through alone.*

The 1975 constitution leaves the system of election to be determined by law, though it does lay down the duration of a parliament, its maximum and minimum size, compulsory voting and, curiously, that "not more than one tenth of the total number of deputies may be elected on the basis of the whole realm being treated as one single constituency, and in proportion to the total percentage of the votes of each party, as the law provides". Under the present law, each administrative division of the country is one constituency (except for the two largest, which are divided), returning from one to twenty-eight members according to electorate. Voting is for a party but the voter may also give a personal vote to one candidate (or two in the largest constituencies); these personal votes are important in deciding which individual candidates are elected. The count takes place in three stages. First, seats are allocated by Droop quota within each constituency (in the five single-member constituencies by relative majority). Any Independent reaching the quota will also be elected. For the second stage the fifty-six constituencies are grouped into nine large ones. In each of these, the seats left unallocated in the first stage are shared proportionally among the parties, subject to certain conditions; the most important of these is that a party must have polled at least 17 per cent of the votes in the whole country. Finally, seats left over are divided among the parties that shared in the second distribution.

In general, the candidates who fill a party's seats are those who have received the largest numbers of personal votes, but there are exceptions. A former prime minister, or the present leader of any party or coalition, is deemed to have received as personal votes the total number of votes cast for his party in that constituency. The voters thus have no power either to express their admiration for such a candidate or to secure his exclusion from parliament.

The results of the two latest elections were:

---

* See AW Gomme, *Greece*, OUP, 1945, p 68 and S Forster, *A Short History of Modern Greece*, Methuen, 2nd edition, 1946, p 164.

	1977			1981		
	votes %	seats	%	votes %	seats	%
New Democracy	41.9	172	57.3	35.9	115	38.3
Socialist (Pasok)	25.3	93	31.0	48.1	172	57.3
Union Dem. Centre	11.9	15	5.0	0.4	—	—
Communist	9.4	11	3.7	10.9	13	4.3
Liberal	1.1	5	1.6	0.4	—	—
Revol. Comm.	0.2	2	0.7	0.1	—	—
National Camp	6.8	2	0.7	—	—	—
Prog. & Left Alliance	2.7	—	—	—	—	—
Progressive	—	—	—	1.7	—	—
Intl Communist	—	—	—	1.4	—	—
others	0.7	—	—	1.1	—	—
totals	100.0	300	100.0	100.0	300	99.9

It will be seen that the weighting of the system has given a substantial advantage to the largest parties and has exaggerated the
change in public opinion; New Democracy lost one seventh of its
votes but one third of its seats. Only three parties secured representation in 1981, and it is reported that the non-representation of
all others is widely felt to be wrong. The new prime minister, Andreas
Papandreou, is of that opinion and wishes to do away with the
weighting.

Greece needs to develop a much greater capacity for co-operation
among her politicians. Proportional representation, by preventing
a large majority for one party, has forced upon the parties some
attempt at co-operation, and the present law provides for parties
to contest an election as a coalition, but it is likely that more progress
would have been made in this direction if the system chosen had
been one less dependent on division into party lists. With the single
transferable vote, some of those parties that appeared as separate
entities might have found expression as wings of one larger party
and the voters could have given expression to the elements of agreement that exist between one party and another.

ISRAEL

The remarks applying to Greece are also pertinent to Israel, which
throughout its existence has used party list proportional representation in its most extreme form – the whole country is one
constituency and the voter has no choice between candidates. A new

country, populated by immigrants from the most diverse backgrounds, is in any case likely to develop a large number of parties, and a party list system does nothing to discourage this tendency, while STV probably would. At least it seems to the outside observer that, for example, the emergence in 1981 of a separate party for Oriental as distinct from European Jews would not have been necessary if people had been able to vote for one of the existing parties while at the same time showing whether they preferred its MPs to be Orientals or Europeans. However, in spite of ethnic, religious and political divisions all cutting across one another, Israel has on the whole formed coalition governments without much difficulty and justified comments such as that of *The Times* on the 1965 election: "It is remarkable that in this young country, whose citizens come from a hundred other countries, so much political consistency should be maintained". The 1981 election gave rise to much less favourable comment, being bitterly contested and giving a very close result, leading to prolonged negotiations giving a second term of office to prime minister Menachem Begin whose past associations with terrorism make him an object of suspicion to many. If such suspicions are justified, it is fortunate that the electoral system denies to the largest party power out of all proportion to its popular support.

party	votes, %	seats won	%
Likud	37.1	48	40.0
Alignment	36.6	47	39.2
Natl Religious	4.9	6	5.0
Agudat Israel	3.7	4	3.3
Democratic Front	3.4	4	3.3
Tehiya	2.3	3	2.5
Tami	2.3	3	2.5
Telem	1.6	2	1.7
Shinui	1.5	2	1.7
Civil Rights	1.4	1	0.8
others (21 lists)	5.2	0	0
totals	100.0	120	100.0

Likud (itself a coalition of earlier parties) formed the government with the support of NRP, Agudat Israel and Tami, holding a total of 61 seats.

There is within Israel dissatisfaction with the impersonality of its party list system, and it must be hoped that this will eventually lead to adoption of a system more likely to promote conciliation.

*

It is surely clear that sweeping generalizations asserting that proportional representation produces evil results such as a multitude of squabbling parties and unstable governments are not justified by experience even with party list forms. What about PR in the only form used in the English-speaking world?

5

Theory and Practice II:
The Voters in Control

What have been the effects in practice of giving representation not to parties but to individual voters?

In different kinds of elections, organized political parties may play the dominant role or a minor one or none; "supervote" is equally applicable to all. In parliamentary elections party is always important and we can draw direct comparisons with those countries already considered where it is made the criterion of seat distribution. As already mentioned*, when the Royal Commission tackled the subject, evidence of the working of the single transferable vote at the parliamentary level was limited to one election in Tasmania. Since then, only a few national parliaments have been added to the system's users but their experience of it has been very long and its use for non-parliamentary bodies has increased enormously, covering the widest imaginable range of organizations. It is high time Britain had another official enquiry to take account of this.

TASMANIA

Much the oldest user of PR/STV is the Australian state of Tasmania, where the Attorney-General, AI Clark†, induced the two towns of Hobart and Launceston to adopt it for electing their town councils and their representatives in the lower house of the state parliament. This lasted only a few years, owing to dissatisfaction, not with PR itself, but with the use of two different systems at the same time. (It was restored in Hobart in 1968.) In 1907 a new electoral act

* p 54.

† The inventor of the chance-free method of transferring a surplus – see p 49.

established PR/STV for the election of the whole lower house and it has remained in force ever since, surviving several attempts to revert to a single-member system or to substitute party lists.

The first election, in 1909, was a triumph over the prophets of doom. Professor Nanson* spoke of it as a complete success, although it had "stood a severe test, for never before in the history of Tasmania had there been so many parties and factions. Yet the result of the election is the rejection of all candidates except Labour and anti-Socialist" – the latter being a cohesive party within which various shades of opinion were represented. The same division has endured to this day, variations in opinion finding sufficient satisfaction in the voters' freedom to discriminate among candidates of the same party. An occasional Independent has been elected and in 1969 one Country party candidate. Unlike those in the other five Australian states, Tasmanian farmers have no need of a separate party to promote their interests, for they can support either of the two existing parties while giving preference to those of its candidates who are farmers. This tendency to produce a very small number of parties is characteristic of STV.

Australian voters in general are strongly regimented by their party organizations but those of Tasmania have long since realized that STV enables them to rebel against party dictation whenever they judge it right to do so. Two instances of this were RD Townley, who in 1946 resigned from the Labour party, stood as an Independent and was elected with more first-preference votes than any other candidate in the state, and his nephew who in 1970 was refused nomination by his party but was easily elected as an Independent. Reading reports of parliamentary debates suggests also that the softening of party lines produced by STV may be responsible for the more civilized language used in Tasmania!

While the British have for far too long tolerated gross anomalies in their election results, Tasmanians have been conscious of minor departures from perfection and, largely through the work of George Howatt, have introduced refinements. The most important change was recommended by the report of a select committee in 1957. The House of Assembly was elected from five 6-member constituencies and this tended to produce deadlock: the two parties were not far from equal in popular support and the election of even numbers of members was liable to make them exactly equal in representation.

---

* The Melbourne *Age*, 8 May 1909.

The simple remedy adopted was to raise the number of members to 35 – 7 from each constituency – thus ensuring that a small majority of votes would secure a majority of one seat. While in the last 6-seat election the two parties secured respectively 50.3 and 43.6 per cent of the votes and 15 seats each, in the first with 7-seat constituencies the figures were 44.5 and 41.1 per cent, 17 and 16 seats (two Independents were also elected). Since that time, Labour has tended to draw further ahead and in 1979 won its third successive election. The figures for this were:

Constituencies		Labour	Liberal	others
Franklin	votes	28,078	15,637	2,476
	seats	4	3	0
Denison	votes	22,825	18,913	3,255
	seats	4	3	0
Bass	votes	22,601	20,083	2,226
	seats	4	3	0
Wilmot	votes	24,446	19,281	396
	seats	4	3	0
Braddon	votes	22,723	17,770	1,235
	seats	4	3	0
totals for state	votes	120,673	91,684	9,588
	%	54.4	41.3	4.3
	seats	20	15	0
	%	57.1	42.9	0

AUSTRALIA

The rest of Australia has been much inclined to electoral experiments, which have been relatively short-lived. The alternative vote has persisted longest, being still in use for the federal House of Representatives and most state parliaments. In the federal Senate elections before 1949, the alternative vote operated in multi-member constituencies; that is, after the first senator had been elected by a clear majority all the papers were counted again to elect the second, again by a clear majority, and so on. The effect of this is that if 51 per cent of the voters vote 1, 2, 3 ... for all the candidates of any one party, that party is bound to take all the seats. In 1949, an increase in the size of the Senate was made the occasion for changing the system of election to PR. This was a reversal of the attitude hitherto taken up by the government party (Labour) and may be accounted for by the fact that it expected in the next election a loss of votes which, under the old system, would have meant the loss of all its seats. Instead of that, the party retained just over its proportional share of the seats for 45 per cent of the votes compared with 52 per cent in the previous election. In the House of Representatives election, taking place at the same time under the alternative vote, it retained only 39 per cent of the seats.

All Australian Senate elections since then have shown a close correspondence between any party's popular support and the seats it wins. This is the more remarkable because of the great differences in size of electorate. Each state is one constituency returning ten senators, half retiring at a time except in the event of a double dissolution in which case all ten are elected together. In addition, the Northern Territory and Papua-New Guinea elect two each. The largest state, New South Wales, has more than ten times the electorate of the smallest, Tasmania. In spite of that, the total party representation is never far from proportional, showing that equality of electorates, though desirable, is far less important than election by quota.

AUSTRALIAN GENERAL ELECTION, 1980

	House of Representatives alternative vote			Senate PR/STV		
	votes, %	seats	%	votes, %	seats	%
Liberal-Country Party	46.3	74	59.2	43.4	15	44.1
Labour	45.1	51	40.8	42.3	15	44.1
Australian Democrat	6.6	—	—	9.3	3	8.8
others	2.0	—	—	5.0	1	2.9
totals	100.0	125	100.0	100.0	34	99.9

The upper house (Legislative Council) in New South Wales is also elected by PR and that of South Australia will be in future. Up to 1975, South Australia elected two members together by the alternative vote, giving extremely distorted results. In the 1968 and 1973 elections, the Labour party actually polled more than half the votes (53 per cent) but won only two and four seats respectively, out of ten! It is not surprising that when a Labour government came to power it took steps to change the system. Long debate led to the institution of a party list proportional system with preferential voting between parties, not candidates, and allocation of the last seat to the largest remainder. The Liberal party objected, especially to this last provision, and when it came to power produced proposals for change. These, however, referred only to the method of counting and retained voting for parties, not persons. Pressure from the Electoral Reform Society of South Australia and from a Liberal member who threatened to cross the floor induced the government to change its mind and from the next election voting will be by STV for individual candidates.

The single transferable vote is also used for many of Australia's local councils; this will be considered further in the section on local government.

MALTA

British governments, however disinclined to reform of the electoral system at home, have usually considered it essential to ensure fair representation for different sections in any of the colonial territories for which they have been responsible. Too often this has meant some such device as separate electorates for different races, but when Malta's constitution was being drawn up in 1921 the Colonial Secretary was LS Amery, who, contrary to the majority of his party, had supported the use of STV to elect the House of Commons. Under his influence STV was incorporated in that constitution and it has survived all subsequent changes, including the granting of independence in 1964. A Royal Commission appointed in 1931 reported that there were no proposals for any change in the voting system, which was "fully understood by the voters and much appreciated by them" and similar opinions have been expressed by leaders of the parties. Only in one respect is understanding obviously incomplete: the two main party organizations urge their supporters to number candidates of their own party *only* – believing, quite wrongly, that to go on to candidates of the other party could help it to win more seats. This makes no difference to the proportional representation of the parties but works against one of the great advantages of STV, its encouragement for the voter to express whatever agreement he may feel with individuals on the other side. When the last candidate of party A is eliminated, this ill-advised instruction results in a huge number of non-transferable votes, which could have been used to decide which of two party B candidates should take the last seat. Within the parties, there is very marked discrimination between candidates, and interest is high, with polls of 90 per cent or more (on a very up to date register) and crowds following the count on screens in the main square of Valetta.

There are at present thirteen 5-member constituencies and the results of the two latest elections were:

| | 1976 | | | 1981 | | |
	votes, %	seats	%	votes, %	seats	%
Labour	51.5	34	52.3	49.1	34	52.3
Nationalist	48.5	31	47.7	50.9	31	47.7
others	0.01			0.01		

The anomalous result of the 1981 election naturally gave rise to much controversy and to suggestions as to how the victory of the party with the fewer votes could be prevented in future. The error is within the margin corresponding to a 5-member constituency, where one sixth of the votes cast may fail to contribute to the election of a member. In all previous elections the number of these "wasted" votes has been roughly equal as between the parties, but in 1981 this was not so: in 9 of the 13 constituencies the last unelected candidate was a Nationalist, their votes totalling 20,207, while in only 4 was it a Labour candidate, that party's "wasted" votes totalling only 8,734.

The anomaly could be corrected by giving effect to those "wasted" votes. The present author has urged that it is undesirable to embark on drastic changes in the electoral law in order to remedy something that has occurred for the first time in 60 years of STV and may not happen again for another 60 years. A simple solution (to be applied only if the party with the most votes loses) would be to award that party enough extra seats (in this instance 4) to bring it up to its proportional number, those seats to be taken by those of its unelected candidates who had the most votes in the last stage of the count.*

It is desirable to keep any such adjustments to a minimum, since they involve counting votes for a party and in Malta there is already far too much emphasis on Party. The electors show a high degree of interest and discriminate sharply between candidates within a party, but they have fallen victim to urging by the party organizations to vote 1, 2, 3, etc. for all of the party's candidates and then stop.

* This is not open to the same objection as the "best losers" variant of the West German system (p 43), since such a candidate would have been chosen by the voters to be the last survivor among several submitted by his party.

That is nonsensical, for a subsequent preference recorded for a candidate of a different party can operate only if there are no longer any candidates of the first party left for it to help – it can affect *which* candidates of the second party are elected but not *how many*. The most serious effect of this instruction is psychological, encouraging voters to look on the other party as an enemy instead of considering possible points of agreement with some of its candidates. That spirit is evident in charges that the 1981 result was due to deliberate gerrymandering – so it may have been but it could also have happened by pure accident. It might be well for Malta to consider abandoning the requirement for equal constituencies, which necessitate frequent boundary revisions, and substitute natural units as permanent constituencies adjusted by increasing or decreasing their number of members.

This unsatisfactory election, with the spate of public controversy to which it has given rise, will have done good if it leads the Maltese people not only to improve the already admirable machinery of their elections but to make much fuller use of the power it places in their hands.

IRELAND – THE REPUBLIC

Much the richest source of information on the working of "supervote" is Ireland, and its history is very interesting.

Although the Royal Commission's report in 1910 failed to persuade enough MPs that the single transferable vote would be the right method for their own election, it did put the idea into the heads of those preparing for other elections. Malta was one example, Ireland another. STV was written into the Act which set up the Irish Free State and those who later campaigned to abolish it liked to say that it had been "imposed" on Ireland by the English. However, a glance at the events of the preceding few years shows that it was by no means imposed against the wishes of the Irish people.

The Proportional Representation Society (which in 1959 became the Electoral Reform Society of Great Britain and Ireland) had members in Ireland, who set up their own separate organization, one of whose activities was to hold a nationwide mock election by STV. This made possible the seizing of an opportunity that arose in 1918 when the town of Sligo, governed by a highly unrepresentative Council, went bankrupt and was taken into commission. There sprang into existence a vigorous Ratepayers' Association, including many members of the hitherto unrepresented minority, whose efforts led to the Sligo Corporation Bill, 1918, and whose provisions included the election of a new council by STV. The election aroused unprecedented interest, with a 73 per cent poll and only 1 per cent of papers spoiled by failure to understand the new system. In every ward, representation was shared fairly among the three parties contesting and (in the two wards where they stood) Independents, and in the West ward a member of both a religious and a political minority, a Protestant Unionist, was elected with nearly twice as many first-preference votes as any other candidate. The overall result was:

	first-preference *votes*	*seats won*
Ratepayers' Association	823	8
Sinn Fein	674	7
Labour	432	5
Independents (2 wards)	279	4

A typical press comment was that of the *Sligo Champion* of the 18 January 1919: "The system has justified its adoption. We saw it work; we saw its simplicity; we saw its unerring honesty to the voter all through; we saw the result in the final count; and we join in the general expression of those who followed it with an intelligent interest – it is as easy as the old way; it is a big improvement and it is absolutely fair".

This success kindled a demand for the same system to be extended to all Irish local authorities, leading to the Local Government (Ireland) Act of 1919 and the holding of elections under it in 1920. One result of these was to demonstrate that the division between Dublin and Belfast was by no means as unqualified as their representation at Westminster made it appear.

	Unionist	*Independent*	*Nationalist*	*Labour*	*Sinn Fein*
DUBLIN MPs	—	—	—	—	7
Councillors	12	2	9	15	42
BELFAST MPs	8	—	1	—	—
Councillors	35	3	5	12	5

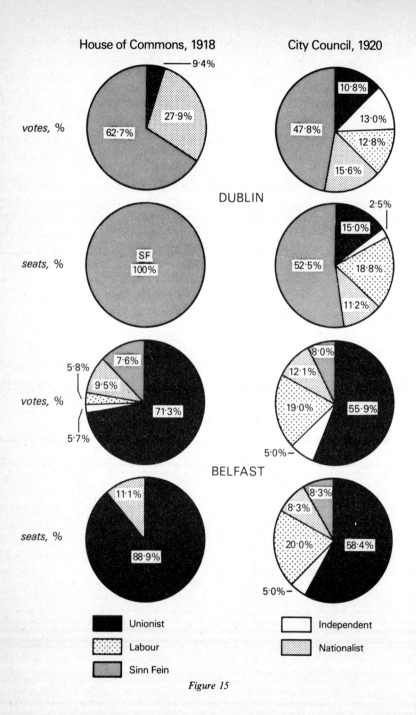

Figure 15

The Unionists, in spite of having won seats in places where they were in a minority, bitterly resented losing the monopoly of their strongholds and expressed their intention of reverting to the old system at the first opportunity; this led the British government to include in its Home Rule Bill a provision that no change must be made for three years.

It was these local government elections which led up to the inclusion, in the Government of Ireland Act, 1920, of provisions that the two Irish parliaments set up under it should be elected by STV (in constituencies returning from 3 to 8 members each) and that no bill to change the system could be tabled until three years after the establishment of the Northern Ireland parliament, until June 1924. The Unionist majority in Northern Ireland did secure a reversion to X-voting (see below, page 94) but what is now the Republic of Ireland has steadily maintained the STV system.

One of its advantages over any other system manifested itself in the very first election to the Dáil in 1922. The Treaty just signed with Britain required an election to be held as soon as possible, in order to give the electors an opportunity of confirming the settlement. As already pointed out*, British elections in comparable circumstances gave the voters no means of showing whether they did or did not wish to accept the Treaty of Rome, but that Irish election made the people's verdict absolutely clear. The leaders of the pro- and anti-Treaty factions came to an agreement to avoid contested elections and nominated an agreed panel of candidates, but an additional 47 candidates presented themselves in defiance of that agreement, thus forcing a contest in three-quarters of the constituencies. The voters there found themselves not limited to electing one Panel candidate (who might be pro- or anti-Treaty) but having a free choice among several Panel candidates, of varying opinions on the Treaty, in addition to non-Panel candidates. Their preference was indisputable: pro-Treaty candidates received 68 per cent of the votes and of the seats. The parties, of course, also secured representation in proportion to their popular support.

In 1937, the Fianna Fáil government of Eamon de Valera wrote into the constitution election of the Dáil by STV, with a minimum constituency size of three members. This was a very important step, since it meant that the system could not be altered except by referendum. The same party, under the same leader, did in fact

*p 45.

attempt to alter it twenty years later, in 1958. When charged with inconsistency, de Valera replied that certain defects, not noticed in 1937, had become apparent – a reasonable answer if he could have produced convincing evidence of those defects. However, at an eve of the poll rally he astonished everyone present by saying that he had to include PR in the constitution "because the people would not have accepted the constitution if I had left it out". Nor would they accept its removal. In spite of the mobilization of all the government's resources, including complete control of one of the three main newspapers, the *Irish Press*, the proposal to change to the British system (called, of course, not that but the "straight vote") was rejected by 486,989 votes to 453,322. The margin being so narrow, Fianna Fáil was tempted to try again, in 1968, but it was then routed by a 3 to 2 majority. Why the difference? Mainly, it seems certain, because in the interval television had appeared, with the result that people who on the first occasion may have seen nothing but highly inaccurate statements in government leaflets and the *Irish Press* were exposed to debates and factual background programmes.

One feature of the first referendum ought to give satisfaction to people on both sides, as it demonstrates the political maturity of the Irish electors. The referendum coincided with a presidential election, in which de Valera was the successful candidate. The YES (for changing the system) side naturally exploited his prestige, and huge posters exhorted people to "vote YES and de Valera". But many thousands voted NO and de Valera. They wanted him for president but were not prepared to follow him in what they had decided was a foolish proposal. This confirms the opinion that STV has an educative effect. X-voting (whether for a person or for a party) asks the minimum of a voter's intelligence; to express degrees of approval for a variety of personalities, policies and parties asks much more and the voter grows accustomed to having more demanded of him. That this is well within the ordinary elector's capacity is demonstrated by the speed with which those new to the system realize and use the power it gives them. One instance is the Treaty issue in the 1922 election; others are discussed below under Northern Ireland.

Most people vote on party lines, with the result that each party wins seats in pretty close proportion to the total of first-preference votes cast for its candidates. Divergences from proportionality are tiny compared with what happens in British elections but for some time past have been increased by the reduction of about half the constituencies to the constitutional minimum of three members. Following a change in the opposite direction (see below p 92) the 1981 election gave a much more accurately proportional result. In all elections there is a very clear reflection of voters' opinions on other matters, of which the most conspicuous is personality. Almost always, the several candidates of any one party in any constituency poll strikingly different numbers of first-preference votes. A party leader normally polls a very large number (indeed he would never have reached the position of leader if the voters had not thus demonstrated their confidence in him) but if he has in any way forfeited their confidence that number will fall sharply in the next election. On the other side of the coin, a person who has been rejected by his party organization may be elected by the voters in defiance of the party. The most conspicuous instance of this is Dr Noel Browne, who is something of a maverick, not fitting permanently into any one party but popular with the voters. In one of his many elections, 1954, he was narrowly defeated as a Fianna Fáil candidate in Dublin South East, and in the next election, 1957, that party refused to nominate him again. He stood as an Independent in the same constituency and was elected ahead of the official FF candidates.

It cannot be expected that party organizations will like that kind of thing, and their wish to control whether a particular individual is elected or not must be a factor in the resistance of British parties to the introduction of STV and in Fianna Fáil's attempts to get rid of it. However, that party now seems to wish to forget those attempts, and during its period of office in 1977–81 actually improved the system by removing a defect in Irish law. Until then, the revision of constituency boundaries had been in the hands of a government department, and each party when in office had tried to manipulate constituencies to its own advantage. Under any proportional system, the scope for this is very small compared with what it is under a majority system, but large parties can obtain a material advantage over small ones by reducing the number of seats per constituency and this did in fact happen. In the 1977 election there were no less than 26 constituencies with the constitutional minimum of only 3 seats each, 10 with 4 members and only 6 with 5. Moreover, all the 9 Dublin constituencies were 3-member, which is indefensible: there are reasonable arguments for them in sparsely populated areas, but not in a congested city. In accordance with a pledge given in the 1977 election, the government put an end to this by handing over

boundary revision to an impartial commission, as in Britain, which
for the 1981 election drew up a very different schedule of constituencies (the total membership of the Dáil being at the same time
raised from 148 to 166). The largest number of members in any
constituency is still 5, but there are now 15 constituencies at that
level, 13 fours and 13 threes. Moreover, none of the boundaries
appeared at all unnatural, and the opposition spokesman supporting
the Electoral Bill said it "was also the first such revision that had
not caused political controversy".*

The result of the 1981 election, with the previous one for com-
parison, was as follows:

	1977			1981		
	1st pref. votes, %	seats	%	1st pref. votes, %	seats	%
Fianna Fáil	50.3	84	57.1	45.3	77*	46.7
Fine Gael	30.9	43	29.3	36.5	65	39.4
Labour	11.6	16*	10.9	9.9	15	9.1
others	7.2	4	2.7	8.3	8	4.8
totals	100.0	147*	100.0	100.0	165*	100.0

* plus the Speaker, by law returned unopposed

In addition to the boundary revision, there were several unusual
features of the 1981 election. One was the advance of Fine Gael under
its dynamic new leader, Dr Garret FitzGerald. He failed in his aim
of supplanting Fianna Fáil as the largest party but, with Labour
support, did have a majority of two seats over FF, and Dr FitzGerald
was elected Taoiseach. In 1973 there had been an explicit coalition
with Labour, each party advising its supporters to give their later
preferences to the other; the result had been a clear majority of votes
and seats for the two parties combined, showing that the resulting
coalition government was the wish of the majority of the nation.
In 1981 there was no such formal arrangement but large numbers
of voters did voluntarily express their support for continuation of
the alliance. However, it fell short of a clear majority in the Dáil
and depended for survival on the eight miscellaneous independents.
Two of these did not enter into the calculation, for they were hunger
strikers imprisoned in Northern Ireland and would not have taken
their seats even if they had been able to do so. An added complication

* Debate on the bill; *Irish Times*, 18 June 1980.

Counterfoil No.	Marcáil ord do rogha sna spáis seo síos. Mark order of preference in spaces below.	Marc Oifigiúil. Official Mark. →
		DOYLE—WORKERS PARTY. (James Doyle, of 10 High Street, Builder.)
		LYNCH—DEMOCRATS. (Jane Ellen Lynch, of 12 Main Street, Grocer.)
		O'BRIAIN—CUMANN NA SAORÁN-ACH. (Séamus O'Briain, ó 10 An tSráid Ard, Oide Scoile.)
		O'BRIEN, EAMON (BARRISTER)—NON-PARTY. (Eamon O'Brien, of 22 Wellclose Place, Barrister.)
		O'BRIEN, EAMON (SOLICITOR)—YOUNG IRELAND. (Eamon O'Brien, of 102 Eaton Brae, Ranelagh, Solicitor.)
		O'CONNOR—NATIONAL LEAGUE. (Charles O'Connor, of 7 Green Street, Gentleman.)
		THOMPSON—FARMERS PARTY. (William Henry Thompson, of Dereen Park, Farmer.)

TREORACHA.

I. Féach chuige go bhfuil an marc oifigiúil ar an bpáipéar.

II. Scríobh an figiúr 1 le hais ainm an chéad iarrthóra is rogha leat, an figiúr 2 le hais do dhara rogha, agus mar sin de.

III. Fill an páipéar ionas nach bhfeicfear do vóta. Taispeáin *cúl an pháipéir* don oifigeach ceannais, agus cuir sa bhosca ballóide é.

INSTRUCTIONS.

I. See that the official mark is on the paper.

II. Write 1 beside the name of the candidate of your first choice, 2 beside your second choice, and so on.

III. Fold the paper to conceal your vote. Show *the back of the paper* to the presiding officer and put it in the ballot box.

(Back of Paper)

No. ....

Election for Constituency of........................ "; and

(k) the deletion of Rules 3 (3), 6 (6) and 6 (7) of the Fourth Schedule.

Figure 16 Irish Ballot Paper

arose when one of these died, creating a casual vacancy in the constituency of Cavan-Monaghan, where in the general election Fianna Fáil polled the most votes. This illustrates the objection to filling such a vacancy by a new election (see page 102) for the likely result of that election would be to render the government's position still more precarious without there having been any movement of public opinion against it. In spite of all this, the government went ahead firmly with its declared policies, and in particular embarked on exploration of possible constitutional changes (requiring the people's consent in a referendum) designed to smooth the path towards improved relations with Northern Ireland.

It was defeated on the budget, causing a general election eight months after the previous one (as in Britain in 1974). This showed a small swing back to Fianna Fáil, which in its turn found itself in office but dependent on support by Sinn Féin the Workers' Party

	1st pref. votes, %	seats	%
Fianna Fáil	47.3	81	49.1
Fine Gael	37.3	63	38.2
Labour	9.1	15	9.1
SFWP	2.3	3	1.8
others	4.0	3*	1.8
totals	100.0	165*	100.0

*plus the Speaker, by law returned unopposed

and Independents. In addition, its leader, Charles Haughey, had to take account of a clear movement of public opinion from his wing of the party to those critical of his leadership – several of these were elected in place of outgoing FF Deputies known as Haughey supporters and his own share of the FF first preference votes in his constituency went down from 85 to 77 per cent. Negotiations between the parties in the light of such indications produced a government with a programme almost certainly commanding the support of the majority of the electors. The most unpopular features of the Fine Gael budget were dropped and Independent plans for measures against inner city dereliction were taken up.

NORTHERN IRELAND

The Unionist majority in Northern Ireland secured a reversion to the single-member, first-past-the-post system in time for the local government elections of 1923 and the election of the provincial parliament in 1929. The motives for this change were never clearly stated and defence of it has usually amounted to no more than an assertion that it made no difference to the representation of the anti-Unionist minority, quoting as proof of this the results of parliamentary elections.

		total seats		Government		
		contested	uncontested	(Unionists)	Opposition	others
PR/STV	1921	52	0	40	12	—
	1925	40	12	37	12	3
majority system	1929	30	22	40	12	—
	1933	19	33	40	12	—
	1938	31	21	41	11	—
	1945	32	20	37	13	2
	1949	32	20	40	12	—
	1953	27	25	39	12	1
	1958	25	27	37	14	1
	1962	28	24	34	17	1
	1965	29	23	37	15	—
	1969	45	7	39	13	—

These figures do indeed show little change, but they are in themselves inconclusive, for they omit all mention of votes cast. For all that the Unionists' publications show, the anti-Unionist vote might have doubled in that period. Of course it has not, because it is less a political vote than a "tribal" one, closely linked to the roughly two to one majority of Protestants over Catholics, which is unlikely to change materially over a few years. Political opinion is most unlikely to have remained for half a century as stable as those figures suggest, and one fact indicates that there was a movement which the X-vote masked. Four members of the Northern Ireland House of Commons at Stormont were elected by the Queen's University, using the single transferable vote, and in them there was a drastic change. In 1921, the Unionist vote in the university was so overwhelming that the party took all the four seats. This preponderance gradually decreased, until in 1962 the Unionists polled only 57 per cent of the votes, winning two seats to one Liberal and one Independent. The same four retained their seats unopposed in 1965, after which the university constituency was abolished, with the creation of four new territorial constituencies.

It seems likely that the true reason for the abolition of PR was that given by Phelim O'Neill in a debate in the Northern Ireland House of Commons on 10 November 1971. This was that "one of the big Unionist party boss men" had found that his popularity with the voters was so low as to put his seat in danger and had therefore insisted on the change to a system which enabled the party to give him a safe seat.

Even if the change of system really did make no difference to the numerical representation of the two "tribes" at Stormont, it did serious harm in other respects. The return to X-voting meant that each party had to select only one candidate in each constituency. Among the Northern Ireland people who wish to remain part of the United Kingdom, some are Catholics, but they are a small minority and it cannot be expected that this overwhelmingly Protestant party will ever select one of them as its sole candidate anywhere, so all MPs on the government side were invariably Protestants, while those on the opposition side were almost invariably Catholics. Hence, every political quarrel became also a religious quarrel and vice versa. Also, while those who wished the province to remain within the UK might have very different views on how it should be governed, the voters had no means of supporting one view or another; they could only vote for the one Unionist candidate where they happened to live. Nor could they express any opinion about any other candidate or party; they were forced to vote as if they thought candidate X was perfect and all others abominable – which is no contribution towards peace in a bitterly divided community.

This absence of power to discriminate between one candidate and another has caused difficulties in other countries using X-voting. In India, the Congress party was formed of people united in their aim of independence from British rule. But when independence was achieved, those same people were far from united on what to do with it. A great party had been built up, needing to fight as one party in order to win power, but to vote Congress no longer signified support for a common policy. The party has split into personal factions. The Scottish National party is in similar trouble, with Left/Right battles for office in its 1981 conference, and so is its Welsh counterpart, Plaid Cymru. As long as no Scottish government exists, Donald Stewart, MP, can go on insisting that "this is not a Socialist party, a Conservative party or any other party – it is a national party"* but if it ever takes office it will have to pursue a Socialist, a Conservative or some other policy. X for an SNP candidate says nothing at all about the voter's wishes in that respect.

Moreover, in Northern Ireland, even though the Unionist/anti-Unionist division was never badly misrepresented at Stormont, the local councils were a very different story. Newspapers reported vehement protests against the abolition of PR, the Catholic minority in many towns found itself with little – or even no – representation on the council, and in Derry the Catholic *majority* came under a Protestant-dominated council. In Belfast, the minority not only lost seats but had their remaining seats confined to the two wards with Catholic majorities – thus emphasizing and exaggerating the hostility between one part of the city and another which has become so notorious. Another great source of ill feeling was the greatly increased scope for gerrymandering. With a proportional system, manipulation of boundaries can affect, at most, only one of the several seats in a constituency; with a majority system it can affect a great many. Even if there is no deliberate intention to rob certain people of their rights, the belief that there is can do almost as much harm. The degree of resentment aroused can be judged from comment in a Co. Londonderry paper, the *Freeman's Journal* of 1 March 1923:

> According to the last census, the total population of Derry city is 40,780, of whom 22,923, or 56.2 per cent, are pro-Free State. [ie anti-Unionist.] A fair system of representation would therefore give the Free Staters approximately 56 per cent of the council's membership. The Belfast parliament had other views, and ordered that for the purposes of the election Derry city should be divided into five wards so drawn that the Free Staters had majorities only in two.... The wards were so arranged that the Free State majority of 56.2 per cent could in no circumstances secure more than 40 per cent of the representation. [In the PR election, 1920, it won 21 seats out of 40.]

Whether that injustice was deliberately engineered or not, it was certainly a reality, and the last election under that X-vote system demonstrates that it could not have been perpetrated if PR had been retained. The city council election of 1968 was a straight fight between Orange (Unionists/Protestants) and Green (Nationalists/

* *The Guardian*, 1 June 1981.

Catholics) and its result is shown in the diagrams in figure 17. It will be noticed that, in addition to their questionable boundaries, the three wards then existing had numbers of councillors by no means proportional to their electorates; the overwhelmingly Green South ward returned only the same number of councillors as did the far smaller North ward with its Orange majority. The net effect was that a 2 to 1 Green majority of votes returned a 12 to 8 Orange majority of councillors. Now suppose that the same people, voting in the same unjust wards, had given the same support to their respective parties but by voting 1, 2, 3 . . . for their candidates instead of X, X, X. . . . The seats in each ward would then have been shared proportionally between Orange and Green, instead of all going to the larger party no matter whether its majority was huge as in South or very small as in North ward. We then find that the result for the whole city would have been exactly reversed – 12 seats to 8 in favour of the majority instead of the minority. As the strictly proportional result would be 13 to 7, all the ingenuity that allegedly went into gerrymandering the wards would have benefited its perpetrators only to the extent of one seat.

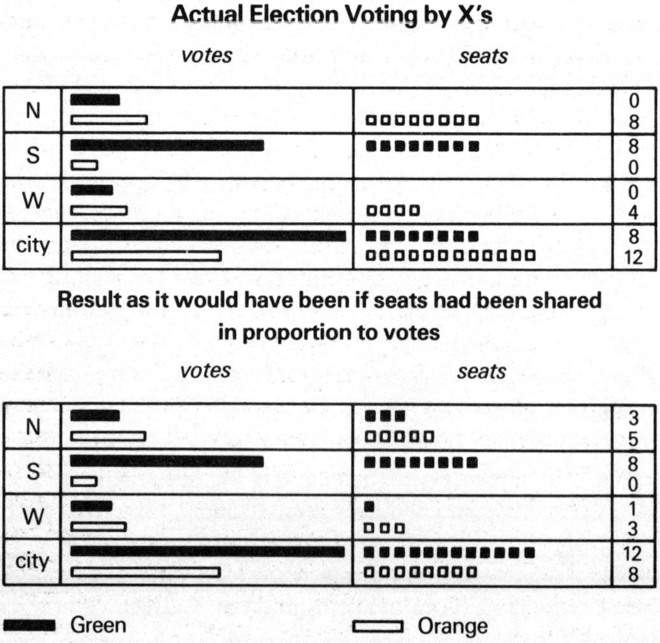

Actual Election Voting by X's

	votes	seats	
N		☐☐☐☐☐☐☐☐	0 / 8
S		■■■■■■■■	8 / 0
W		☐☐☐☐	0 / 4
city		■■■■■■■■ ☐☐☐☐☐☐☐☐☐☐☐☐	8 / 12

Result as it would have been if seats had been shared in proportion to votes

	votes	seats	
N		■■■ ☐☐☐☐☐	3 / 5
S		■■■■■■■■	8 / 0
W		■ ☐☐☐	1 / 3
city		■■■■■■■■■■■■ ☐☐☐☐☐☐☐☐	12 / 8

■■■ Green   ☐☐☐ Orange

Figure 17 Derry City Council Election, 1968

The use of X-voting for fifty years is undoubtedly one reason why relations between the religious communities have been so much worse in Northern Ireland than in the Republic. (Not the only reason; the minority is much larger, and therefore more plausibly to be feared.) The Protestant minority in the Republic has never needed to associate itself with any particular party and has always had its spokesmen on the Government as well as the Opposition benches. It pays any party to widen its appeal by selecting candidates of both religious persuasions, and any elector wishing to be represented by someone of his own faith can promote that by giving such a candidate preference over others of the same party. When violence erupted in the north in 1968, the reaction of ordinary people south of the border was one of horrified astonishment, and that this was occurring under the "straight vote" was one of the reasons for the decisive rejection of that system in the referendum.

The Electoral Reform Society worked for many years to get PR restored in Northern Ireland, and eventually the British government became convinced that, however desirable X-voting was thought to be for the British parliament, it was too dangerous in the different circumstances of Northern Ireland. By 1972 the demand for PR had become virtually unanimous on the non-Unionist side, and the British government, with the support of the Opposition, took urgent measures to accede to it. The Stormont parliament had already been suspended and it was now to be replaced by a 78-member Assembly, elected by STV. New district councils were also to be elected, their poll being in May 1973 with the Assembly following in June. A boundary commission had already drawn single-member wards for the new district councils, but there was no difficulty in combining these into larger ones, each electing from 4 to 8 councillors; for the Assembly time was saved by using the 12 existing constituencies that each returned one MP to Westminster. These elected from 5 to 8 members each, according to electorate. Returning officers and their staffs were trained by the Electoral Reform Society and the government used all the publicity media for instructing voters. Both elections went smoothly, with a good turnout and few spoiled papers, and it was remarkable how quickly the voters realized their new powers and used them. The vast majority were still polarized between Orange and Green, but they could now distinguish between different shades of their colour and did so, particularly between moderates who wished to accept the government's proposals for power-sharing between majority and minority and the hard-liners who did not. The balance of public opinion was clearly for power-sharing and an embryonic power-sharing Executive was formed at the beginning of 1974. Consternation was caused to this Executive by the calling of a British general election – under X-vote of course – for February. The hard-line Unionists, who thought it a law of nature that the majority should rule alone and who were additionally incensed by the conference at Sunningdale which went rather ahead of public opinion in seeking co-operation with the Republic, were determined to end this experiment. The Westminster election played into their hands by giving them 11 out of the 12 seats for only 51 per cent of the votes – encouraging them to behave as if they had the support of eleven twelfths of the electors. They organized a strike which forced the abandonment of the power-sharing experiment and Northern Ireland is still under direct rule from Westminster. Fortunately, this did not prevent the district council elections from being held again under STV in 1977 and 1981, but the continued failure to find a solution at provincial level has led to increasing polarization, involving in 1981 the loss of his seat by Gerry Fitt, the former Social Democratic and Labour party leader, and large gains for Ian Paisley's party at the expense of the more moderate Official Unionists. Even so, Paisley's DUP has overall control of only 1 out of the 26 councils, which is very different from what would probably have happened under X-voting.

STV in local government is discussed further in the next chapter.

THE UNIVERSITIES

Following a recommendation of the Speaker's Conference, supporters of PR/STV secured its inclusion in the Representation of the People bill, 1917, and the vital clauses were very narrowly defeated on a free vote. On an amendment concerning instructions to the boundary commissioners, the figures were:

	for PR	*against PR*
Liberals	76	53
Conservatives	38	84
Labour	13	10
Irish Nationalists	14	1
totals	141	148

There remained, however, a clause establishing STV for those university constituencies which returned more than one member – Oxford, Cambridge and the Combined English Universities, two each, and the Scottish Universities, three. If fair representation of the political parties were the main consideration, this would have been of little value, the numbers being too small, but the effects in other respects were dramatic and highly beneficial.

Before 1918, Oxford and Cambridge had been Conservative pocket boroughs, any two men whom the party chose to nominate being sure of election. In the eight elections from 1885 to 1910, there was only once even a contest – in Cambridge in 1906 when there were three Conservative candidates. From 1918 onwards, elections were nearly always contested, and although the complexion of the voters remained predominantly Conservative it became plain that if the party wished to hold the seats it must select candidates who were personally worth voting for. Already in the second election, 1922, one of the two Cambridge MPs was an Independent, and a tradition gradually grew up that university MPs ought to be independent. The effect of personality was clearly seen in the Oxford election of 1935, when one Conservative candidate was the highly respected MP of twenty-five years' standing, Lord Hugh Cecil, and the other was the relatively unknown Professor Cruttwell. Had voting still been by two X's, it is certain that most Conservatives would have voted for both of them, so that both would have been elected, with nearly equal votes. However, when those same people had to express a preference between the two Conservatives, most of them chose their distinguished sitting member, with the result that he romped home with 7,365 first-preference votes (nearly half as many again as the quota) to Cruttwell's 1,803, the Independent candidate AP Herbert having 3,390 and JL Stocks, Labour, 2,683. Cecil's 2,284 surplus naturally went mainly to Cruttwell, leaving him nearly equal with Herbert, with Stocks at the bottom being eliminated. By nearly eight to one, Stocks' supporters preferred Herbert to Cruttwell, so he was elected to the second seat.

One of the most distinguished of women MPs, Eleanor Rathbone, had failed in 1922 to win a seat in her own city of Liverpool, polling 40 per cent of the votes in a straight fight. In 1929, 34 per cent of the votes secured for her one of the two seats in the Combined English Universities. The by-election caused by her death in 1946 is also of interest, since it illustrates a defect in the 1918 Act. This omitted to make any provision for by-elections, so when that 2-member constituency had to fill one casual vacancy X-voting was used. Aspirants for that vacancy appear not to have allowed for the vote not being transferable, so there were three Independent candidates, one Conservative and one British People's Party and the Conservative was elected with 5,483 votes against 12,805 for his four opponents combined. Since the background of all three Independents was decidedly Left rather than Right, it is certain that transfers of votes would have elected one of them instead of the Conservative.

In the Queen's University, Belfast, we have an interesting contrast between the election of its one Westminster MP and that of its four members at Stormont. The former automatically returned a Unionist, with others in so hopeless a position that they seldom considered it worth while to present a candidate; the latter were nearly always contested and gave a true reflection of the changing opinions of the graduates (see page 95). This effect of STV made the election far more interesting, and we have a measure of this interest in the difference in turnout. In the X-vote Westminster election in 1945, only 51 per cent of the graduates voted, compared with an average of 65 per cent for the rest of Northern Ireland, but in the STV election of their four Stormont members in 1949 76 per cent voted, which was only 1 per cent below the average for the whole province in that election. That is, the free choice of candidates, and the knowledge that the choice expressed would affect the result, appears to have stimulated voting sufficiently to offset the depression of the poll by exclusively postal voting.

The by-election caused by Eleanor Rathbone's death draws attention to the question of how best to fill a casual vacancy. This is of small importance compared with the election of a whole parliament, but objectors to proportional systems often raise it as a difficulty. In the Combined Universities election, if the vote had still been transferable as it was in the original election of the two members, the new MP would have been incontestably the choice of the majority. The objection is, of course, that if the deceased member happened to represent a minority, that minority will lose its representation.

To give some chance for the minority to retain its representation, the multi-member constituency might be divided, for by-election purposes only, into single-member ones, each MP choosing to associate himself for that purpose with one of these. If his support was highly concentrated in that area, a person of similar views would stand a chance of succeeding him. However, it is only a chance and the method has not so far been thought worth trying. The alternative adopted in most countries with proportional systems is to abandon the idea of a new election and fill the vacancy on the basis of the original votes. With an ordered party list system, this will mean co-opting the person who appeared next on the same list as the deceased member. If the voter had a substantial say in choosing which persons were elected (e.g. in Belgium), he will have been asked in the general election to vote also for a number of *suppléants* who will stand ready to fill any casual vacancy that may arise in their party.

With the single transferable vote, voluntary organizations are often content simply to co-opt the "runner-up" in the original election. Where voting is overwhelmingly on purely personal lines, this is acceptable, but it clearly would not do in a party political election, where the deceased member might be, for instance, left-wing Labour and the "runner up" a right-wing Conservative – or vice versa. The answer to this is to re-count the original ballot papers so that the voters who have lost their representative elect his successor from among the non-elected candidates. (This has the incidental advantage of probably widening the voters' choice by encouraging each party to nominate an additional candidate in case he may be needed to fill a casual vacancy.) This method is used in Tasmania and Malta. There are variations of detail which do not affect the essential principle, and there has to be provision for what is to happen if any of the original candidates are no longer available.

There is no perfect way of electing only one person, and which of these methods is chosen will depend largely on the relative importance attached to preserving the original fair representation or to providing a new test of public opinion. The latter is much less needed under PR, since the elected body is representative to start with and requires no correction unless there has been an unusually large movement of public opinion. In Britain, by-elections do serve a useful purpose by enabling voters to protest against something which most of them did not want in the first place.

6

Local Government

GREAT BRITAIN

As already mentioned*, PR in Ireland began with local government. In British conditions at least, this would be a very suitable field for experiment, for several reasons.

First, while many people genuinely believe that it is necessary for the good government of a country to have one party with a working majority in parliament, even if no one party has won the support of a majority of the voters, far fewer hold that belief about local government; on the contrary, many citizens feel that the national parties are rather out of place in local government; they want the most suitable people as councillors rather than party rule. The fear that PR might lead to a multiplicity of parties and no one of them in control has little relevance where the town hall is concerned. Second, there are many wards and parishes which elect several councillors together; for these, the only change needed is to vote 1, 2, 3 ... instead of X, X, X.... The quite understandable hesitation to accept a larger electoral area does not apply. An additional advantage is that experiments with different electoral systems can be made on any scale, from one parish council upwards.

Attempts to persuade parliament to allow such experiments have so far failed. While bills making the change mandatory have been opposed on the ground that they were too wholesale, those making it permissive were opposed on the ground that we could not have different places using different systems. That was said even in relation to the new Greater London Council, although this already differed

*p 87.

in many ways from all other councils. It would be possible for a local authority to promote a private bill (or to include an additional clause in a bill already being promoted for other purposes) giving it power to change the way in which it is elected, but this has not yet happened. The only successes have been two relating to bodies that no longer exist as separately elected authorities.

A private member, Lord Frederick Cavendish, secured the inclusion in the Education Act, 1870, of the cumulative vote for the election of school boards. Although the cumulative vote is uncertain in its operation,* it did in practice give reasonably fair representation of the main parties and did enable the occasional Independent to be elected. Several witnesses before a select committee of the House of Commons testified that minority representation greatly facilitated the working of the Act, and a Royal Commission reporting on the Elementary Education Acts in 1888 strongly advised its retention.

The Scottish Education Act, 1918, set up new education authorities to be elected by the single transferable vote. Four elections of these authorities took place, after which, in 1929, their functions were transferred to the county councils. STV was the method chosen, because it was recognized as essential that different religious views should be represented, experience of the cumulative vote had not given complete satisfaction, and STV had been brought to public notice at that time by the Sligo election, the favourable report of the 1917 Speaker's Conference and the activities of the Proportional Representation Society, which had a vigorous branch in Scotland and whose secretary, John H Humphreys, played a large part in explaining the system to electors and returning officers.

There were 38 authorities, with a total membership of 987. They were elected in constituencies each returning from 3 to 10 members; small authorities were not divided and there were no arbitrary boundaries. Instruction of the voters had to be done in the few weeks between publication of the regulations and polling day and was carried out by newspaper and cinema publicity, PR Society leaflets, public meetings and demonstrations. According to the efficiency of the local arrangements, ballot papers spoiled by failure to understand the system varied from under 1 per cent to over 3 per cent. The returning officers had no difficulty. Polls were low, but no worse than in most British local government elections.

The elections certainly attained their objects. The very great

---

* See p 29.

majority of those who voted elected a man or woman of their choice, and all important sections of opinion were represented fairly. (Some Protestants complained that too many Roman Catholics were elected in proportion to their numbers in the population, but the *Glasgow Herald*, 7 June 1919, rightly reproved them for having been less keen to cast their votes.) A typical result was that for the second division of Renfrewshire in 1925. There were 9 seats to be filled and 13,306 valid votes, so the quota was 1,331.

	first-preference votes	quotas obtained	seats won
Moderates	9,936	7 + 619 votes over	7
Roman Catholics	3,272	2 + 610 votes over	2
Labour	98	0 + 98 votes over	0

In the same election the total result for the seven divisions of Glasgow was:

	first-preference votes	seats won	seats in proportion to votes
Moderates	130,115	28	27.8
Roman Catholics	53,929	12	11.5
Labour	26,587	5	5.7
Independent	90	0	—

This may be compared with the result of X-voting in the first election of the Strathclyde Regional Council in 1974:

	votes	seats won	seats in proportion to votes
Labour	388,480	68 + 3 unopp.	44.0
Conservative	253,312	21	28.7
Scot. Nat.	130,126	5	14.8
Liberal	39,839	2	4.5
others	70,995	4	8.0
totals	882,752	100 + 3 unopp.	100.0

Not only is reform easier to introduce at the local than at the parliamentary level, but also the case for it is much more obvious. Because the parties are unevenly distributed over the country, there has never been a House of Commons composed of one party only, but in the smaller area covered by a local authority it may happen that the same party is the largest in every ward. There are, in fact, in nearly every round of local elections, a few one-party councils. In a much larger number the "opposition" is so small as to be quite incapable of manning all the committees or supplying effective criticism. It is noticeable that where there have been serious charges of corruption they have related to councils in which that position exists. London especially has often produced one-party borough councils, and although none arose from the last election in 1978 there were several that barely escaped a clean sweep – for instance Hackney with 59 Labour councillors out of 60 and Kingston upon Thames with 44 Conservatives out of 50.

Changes in public opinion are likely to be exaggerated even more than in parliamentary elections, often involving the loss of valuable, experienced councillors, since the same few people changing sides may unseat not merely one MP but several councillors. One example out of many is the Bedford ward of Wandsworth, where in two consecutive elections the votes for the three candidates of each of the two main parties were:

| | 1974 | | 1978 | |
	Labour	Conservative	Labour	Conservative
	1,507	1,374	1,909	2,223
	1,494	1,287	1,821	2,180
	1,375	1,249	1,764	2,163
total votes	4,376	3,910	5,494	6,566
seats won	3	0	0	3

Clearly it would have been much more in accordance with the voters' wishes if in 1974 the Labour majority had elected two councillors and the Conservative minority one, and if the swing to the Conservatives in 1978 had given them one additional seat at the expense of the one less popular Labour councillor.

Another borough, Camden, had all three of its representatives on the Greater London Council changed from Labour in 1964 to Conservative in 1967 although only about one voter in twelve changed sides, and in the next election, 1970, a still smaller swing put them back to all Labour. In the London borough council elections of 1968 there was a real, and unusually large, swing of votes from Labour to Conservative, but it was magnified out of all proportion in the seats. Hillingdon, which had been Labour controlled, found itself with a 100 per cent Conservative council.

The most conspicuous example is Islington, which had a Labour-controlled borough council for 34 years and for 15 years 100 per cent Labour representation at all levels – borough, county and parliamentary – although the Conservative voters amounted to about one third of the whole. In 1968, the Conservatives increased their vote to just over half the total and took 47 out of the 60 seats. Only two of their councillors had had any local government experience, and in 1971 they all lost their seats again. This is not conducive to good government. Neither does it even benefit the dominant party, which, in the absence of an opposition party to criticize its actions, has developed opposing factions within itself. In 1981 this "opposition" defected to the Social Democrats.

Multi-member wards also bring to light what is not obvious in our parliamentary constituencies: the impersonality of the X-vote. It is possible for our present prime minister to believe that the 20,918 X's cast for her as the one Conservative candidate in Finchley are some indication of her personal popularity; it is not possible for anyone to believe that the votes cast for the three Conservative councillors in the Friern Barnet ward of the same borough tell us anything about the voters' opinions of them personally:

Burton, David	2,856
Tiplady, John	2,831
Gibson, Frank	2,827

There must be far more than 29 Conservative voters who think one of their candidates better fitted than another to look after the welfare of the borough, but they cannot show it except by depriving their party of either one or two votes. If they want to give their party full support, they must vote X, X, X for all its three candidates – three equal X's however unequal in personal qualities they may be. It is true that voters, especially in the big towns, do use a local election as an opportunity to express their opinion of the national parties – particularly of an unpopular government – but this does not mean that they would not welcome an opportunity to express also their views on which candidates would make the most competent councillors, which have the best ideas about housing, schools, traffic problems or whatever.

A small experiment in my own town of Tunbridge Wells suggests that indeed they would. People who had just voted with X's for three councillors were invited to vote again by numbers among the same nine candidates. The party balance among those taking part (11:6:3) was not very different from that in the entire ward (16:7:3), so presumably they were a reasonably representative sample, but in other respects the differences were striking. The first contrast appeared on the counting of first-preference votes.

	X	STV		*X*	STV		*X*	STV
Conservative			Liberal			Labour		
Spare	927	90	Morris	399	26	Headdon, W	171	11
Streeten, Mrs	906	35	Rees	384	17	Lewis, Mrs	169	6
Woodland	881	17	Hart, Mrs	377	35	Headdon, Mrs E	158	22

Instead of near equality among the candidates of any one party there were marked differences. The only unsatisfactory feature of the STV result was an apparent tendency to alphabetical voting – which would not be surprising in people suddenly asked without any preparation to use an unfamiliar system. However, this cannot be the whole explanation of the lead shown by the candidate whose name appeared first among those of his party, for that lead is by far the largest in the case of the candidate who was easily the best known – Spare had recently been a very popular mayor. The transfers were mainly on party lines, so that the Conservatives elected two councillors (instead of all three) and the Liberals one. The Labour voters were too few to elect one councillor out of three (they would of course have elected one in a 6-member ward) but their votes were not entirely without effect, for the transfers from the last eliminated Labour candidate helped to decide between two Liberals who were neck and neck – and most of the votes from a Labour woman went to the Liberal woman.

Whatever may be the voters' reasons for giving preference to one candidate over another, it is those preferences which decide who is elected. This means that even if opinions on local issues are over-shadowed by national party allegiance, opinion on those local issues is nevertheless represented. A recent case of local controversy cutting across party lines occurred in the Dublin city council election of 1979. The majority of the outgoing council wished to develop the site of the earliest Viking settlement; the site was occupied by protesting squatters and its preservation became a major election issue. Within each party, preservationist candidates fared best (the lord mayor being ousted by a preservationist woman of his own party), and Independents and small parties fighting specifically on that issue

greatly increased their votes, resulting in a 25 to 20 majority of the
new council against development.

The effect of being able to vote on more than one kind of question
at the same time has been conspicuous in Northern Ireland, where,
when STV was restored after fifty years of X-voting, the first elections
to be held were those for district councils, in May 1973. The voters
were quick to realize and to use their power to select the most
suitable individuals and reject those they considered unsuitable (even
if, as in one case, this was the local party boss!) and this diversion
of attention towards the real functions of the council and away from
tribal warfare between Protestants and Catholics produced an
immediate improvement in the atmosphere.

> Dr Ray McClean of the Social Democratic and Labour party thinks that
> Derry should have a running track of international standard. Mr Jack
> Allen, of the United Loyalist group, thinks on the other hand that
> Londonderry should have a running track of international standard. As
> chairman and deputy chairman respectively of the new Londonderry
> council they have tacitly agreed to shelve the Derry/Londonderry issue
> while they get on with the site for the running track.*

While it cannot be claimed that all is now sweetness and light,
councillors are devoting much more energy to using their limited
powers to the general good and less to fighting each other; rotation
of chairmanships between the two communities has become normal,
and Belfast has seen the previously inconceivable phenomenon of
a non-Unionist lord mayor married to a Catholic, while one of his
successors, who in 1973 seemed to be a hard-line Unionist, is now
busy cultivating friendly relations with Dublin.

Multiple-X voting has the opposite effect, directing electors'
attention more and more to their party divisions and away from
consideration of local questions. A ludicrous example of blind party
voting occurred in the election of two councillors for one ward of
Tunbridge Wells in 1976, when one of the two Labour candidates
realized, too late to withdraw, that he was under age. The local
paper gave great prominence to his appeal, "Please don't vote for
me", but 175 people did. And how many for the other Labour
candidate? 176. Block voting for a party, obscuring the voters' wishes
about local matters, can do great harm to a town. Since a party's

* Gillian Linscott, *The Guardian*, 5 July 1973.

supporters have no means of discriminating between those of its candidates who hold different views on, say, a town centre development plan, a council may well embark on irreversible changes contrary to the wishes of the majority of its electors. Changes of the party in control may mean repeated wasteful reversals of policy, with those affected unable to plan ahead. In Tameside (a Greater Manchester metropolitan district which elects one third of its council each year) the Conservatives made large gains in 1975 and further gains in 1976 which gave them control, whereupon they claimed a mandate for halting the previously Labour-controlled council's far advanced plans for comprehensive education. This not only put the council in dispute with the government, but left pupils, teachers and parents in great uncertainty. There was really no clear "mandate" either for or against comprehensive schools, for there is no means of knowing how many of those who voted for either party did so because of or in spite of its policy on education. If anything, the 1975 and 1976 elections would seem to suggest a movement of public opinion away from the Conservative policy, for although they won in both years their percentage of the vote declined from 53 to 50 while Labour's rose from 39 to 43.

The over-emphasis on party has deplorable effects on the parties themselves and their councillors. There is often an excess of party discipline, all councillors of a given party being expected to vote together even when the subject of the vote is a purely administrative matter, unconnected with the party's principles. There have been cases, in each of the two largest parties, of a newly-elected councillor being required to sign a letter of resignation, to be used against him if he fails to obey the party whip. Usually, councillors draw the line at dictation by any outside body, but even that is sometimes attempted. In 1980, an influential group in the Bristol District Labour party drew up proposals which included:

All local policy should be determined by the District Labour party and made binding on the Labour group in the council.

All group officers ... should be elected by a joint meeting of the district party and the Labour group.

The district party should take over all responsibility for maintaining group discipline in the town hall. The imposition of penalties on councillors would be by a secret ballot of the local general committee.*

* Paul Keel, *The Guardian*, 24 November 1980.

The spirit of which those proposals are an extreme example, can lead to serious misgovernment. However undesirable, dictation by one party is at least practicable when that party has a clear majority on the council. When it has not, attempted dictation simply will not work. The position demands some form of co-operation between people of different parties, but the traditions that have been built up are all against this. People who have been fighting each other in efforts to monopolize the council, who have been denouncing the other side as people unfit to be trusted with running the town, cannot easily adapt themselves to compromise with the "enemy". The most notorious example of the harm done is the city of Liverpool, which over several elections has had a fluctuating three-party balance. Its problems of unemployment, bad housing, etc. are enough to test the competence of any council, but much of the energy that should have gone into their solution has been wasted on internal wrangling. Real work has been hampered by such things as refusal of the largest party to co-operate unless it is given all the committee chairmanships. There must be thousands of citizens who would like to kick out any councillors who seem to be more concerned with their own and their party's ambitions than with the city's welfare, and to elect only men and women of proven concern for their fellow-citizens, but they in their turn are hampered by the X-vote which allows them no choice between one individual and another of the same party.

On councils with an assured majority for one party, the effects of X-voting are different but no less serious. The lack of an effectively critical opposition may conceal inefficiency, extravagance or even corruption. Unrepresented minorities lose hope of being listened to.

County councils that are nearly all of one party may show a lack of consideration for the district councils below them, neglecting to pass on information important to the district or demanding action to an impracticable timetable. People with talents that could be of great value to the community are lost to the council because they do not belong to the dominant party. An analysis of Kent County Council elections since the last war* shows that the Labour party, although always supported by between one quarter and nearly one half of the voters, has had representation fluctuating over a much wider range, from 41 per cent in its best year down to 3 per cent in its worst, with never a consistent growth or decline. The Conservatives, with between 49 and 64 per cent of the votes, have had from 56 to

---

* Eric M Syddique, *Representation*, Summer 1980, p 26.

97 per cent of the seats. Labour strength is greatest in the industrial areas to the north of the county, but is not sufficiently concentrated to give it safe seats there; hence it has been impossible for the party to build up an experienced team of councillors to monitor the Council's work effectively.

AUSTRALIA

Some other countries, especially Australia, have been much more ready than Britain is to experiment with different methods of election; New South Wales is a particularly rich source of information on how they have worked. X-voting is now extinct in Australia and since 1893 has gradually been replaced by various forms of preferential voting. In New South Wales before 1953 most local councils were elected by the block vote, i.e. using as many X's as there were vacancies. This was replaced by the single transferable vote until in 1968 an amendment to the Act substituted majority preferential voting; that is, the ballot papers were counted so as to elect the first representative by a clear majority, counted again to elect the second in the same way, and so on for as many seats as had to be filled. (The former Australian Senate system.) However, councils were allowed to hold polls for STV and twenty authorities did so. In 1976 there was a general return to STV, wherever there were three or more seats to be filled.

The Proportional Representation Society of Australia has studied the effects of the different systems, with the results that might be expected. With X-voting there was the usual tendency for elections to be contested by the national parties or by locally-organized groups and for the largest of these in any one electoral district to win all the seats. Majority-preferential voting made no difference to this pattern except to make sure that the party sweeping the board was one with an overall majority, but it emphasized the absurdities of the system, drawing attention to the fact that many of those elected had far less personal support than some of those defeated. In a multiple-X election the last person elected usually has nearly as many X's as the first, but with the multiple alternative vote he will have started with very few first-preference votes (and probably very few seconds either), far behind not only the most popular candidate of his own party but also candidates of opposing parties. In such an election it is common for the same person to be the runner-up every time, never being elected although he may be the second most popular. It is not surprising that one experience of this was enough for some municipalities, which by referendum reverted to quota-preferential voting (STV), or that the system was abandoned completely after three elections. An incidental drawback is the length of time taken by the count; in one New South Wales example this was found to be fourteen times what would have been needed for counting by STV.

The best documented example of the use of STV for local government elections in Australia is the town of Armidale. An Act of 1919 allowed a poll on the subject to be taken on the petition of one-fifth of the voters, and Armidale took advantage of this in 1928, before extensions of the franchise made the one-fifth an impracticable target for other towns. STV has been in use ever since, apart from the short break enforced by the 1968 amendment. Before 1928 the council elections were dominated by party tickets, one or other of which usually swept the board; after 1928 the power of these party groups disappeared and members (known as Aldermen) were elected on their individual merits. One member, Dr Ellen Kent-Hughes, said that

> the Armidale system made it possible to keep party politics out. Aldermen here are elected as individuals and not as party nominees. They vote according to their judgment as to what is best for the city, not in accordance with political party dictates or party considerations. We don't get the party squabbles in this council that are found in other councils of the state.*

However, big party organizations cannot be expected to welcome this, and in several instances their opposition has secured a reversion to majority voting. This has happened in places where a poll of the electors was required, but does not necessarily mean that the electors were dissatisfied with STV. It will be recalled that such a move by the Irish government in 1958 very nearly succeeded – by giving the X-vote an attractive name, "straight vote" (carefully avoiding calling it the English system!) and putting out a series of highly misleading statements such as that "the straight vote means the majority wins", relying on the Irish public not to know that nearly all British governments are elected by a minority. In the second referendum in 1968, when television had arrived and put both sides of the argument

---

* George Howatt, *National Municipal Review*, 1956, p. 187.

objectively, the better-informed electorate voted overwhelmingly to retain PR.

UNITED STATES

Similar unscrupulous tactics did succeed in New York city in 1947. The highly organized and wealthy Tammany Hall* (which spent $35,000 on its campaign against $4,000 by the Keep Proportional Representation Committee) made much use of the fact that in the previous election two Communists had been returned. This was only 7 per cent of the council, representing the same proportion of first-preference votes, and both were councillors of high quality, one being a black lawyer generally regarded as the leading representative of his community in the city. Both had been re-elected in 1945, but in the changed atmosphere two years later it was possible to use them to work up a red scare and the campaign to repeal PR succeeded after two failures. The same kind of thing has happened in a number of other American cities, the only survivor at present being Cambridge, Massachusetts.

Nobody has been able to produce any evidence that PR has worked against the interests of the citizens generally – only against those of the dominant party machine. In New York, the last pre-PR election gave the Democrats, with only a few more votes than the Republicans, seven seats to the Republicans' two (with none for anyone else). PR of course reduced the majority to its proper size, with a healthy opposition, while reversion to X-voting has restored the former steam-roller majorities (e.g. 32 to 6 in the 1965 election). This would not matter so much if the council members on each side were not "lobby-fodder" owing their seats to their respective party machines. When they owed their seats to the preference of the *voters* for them over other candidates of the same party, and when a few were not even party nominees at all, they were likely to be more reliable guardians of the citizens' interests. There are also serious allegations of gerrymandering – which of course would be impossible if each borough were still one PR constituency. No less serious than the mis-representation of parties is the under-representation of ethnic minorities. A black is automatically elected for Harlem but has little

---

*Headquarters of the Democratic Party Organization in New York; hence the organization itself, which found its power broken by STV.

chance elsewhere in the city, and a Puerto Rican still less. Those two groups together amount to over one quarter of New York's population but have less than a tenth of the council seats – hardly a contribution to the solution of racial problems. During the PR era, ethnic representation was much more equitable but without any noticeable tendency for voters to divide on those lines. A voter would give preference to a black, a Jew, an Italian or whatever among the candidates of his party but would usually go on to other candidates of the same party; very few continued to blacks, Jews or Italians of other parties. The same happened when STV was restored to school board elections; see p 139.

Has either system brought New York better government? The answer must be largely subjective, but there can be few to argue that New York since 1947 has been a model of good government. Remembering that Sligo turned to PR as a remedy for its bankrupt state, perhaps New York should look again at that example.

CANADA

Canada also has had considerable experience of the single transferable vote at city and provincial level, but two recent official enquiries, one by the federal government* and one in Quebec, have entirely ignored it, discussing only the proportional representation of parties. It is difficult to think of any excuse for this omission.

Some of the applications of STV lasted only a short time, and possibly the enquirers may have accepted this too readily as proof of its unsuitability. This is a superficial view, for it ignores other instances where STV has been used over long periods and does not discuss whether the reasons for its abandonment were sound. In some places there was admittedly inadequate preparation of the electorate, and there may have been vested interests prevailing over the wider interests of the community.

The brief applications occurred in the first quarter of the twentieth century and are discussed by Hoag and Hallett,† from whose work the following quotations are taken. Experience of STV covered "at least 60 separate elections of city councils as well as a large number of elections of ... municipal boards". In British Columbia,

* Pepin-Robarts Task Force on National Unity; report, January 1979.

† Clarence G Hoag and George H Hallett, Jr, *Proportional Representation*, Macmillan, New York, 1926, pp 223–234.

public spirited citizens ... secured the adoption of PR by the two large cities of the province and by several smaller communities. They had neither the time nor the energy, however, to combat effectively the determined attacks which were made by politicians as soon as they awoke to the possibilities of the new system, or to spread an understanding of the significance of the change in the smaller places where conditions had been fairly satisfactory under the old system. Before it was fully understood, therefore, PR was abolished by popular vote in Victoria and Vancouver and by action of the local councils in New Westminster, Nelson, Port Coquitlam and the rural district of Mission. In the three elections in which PR was used in Vancouver, it added to the council one of the city's leading businessmen and gave organized labour representatives on the city council and on the school board, which it had never had before.

The Vancouver *Province*, though opposed to PR, noted the improved temper of the elections and the high turnout. The Vancouver *Daily World* noted as one of the benefits of PR the fair representation of different geographical areas within West Vancouver.

On Saskatchewan: "In Regina its adoption was followed by a marked increase in voting, indicating an increasing interest in civic affairs." In Saskatoon the city clerk reported great interest and very favourable opinions on the quality of the council. "The whole proceeding ... worked very satisfactorily." Similar opinions were expressed by the city clerks of the two other cities involved.

Why were these apparently promising experiments abandoned so quickly? As in New York and elsewhere, the answer would appear to lie in the opposition of powerful organizations to a system that prevents any one of them from monopolizing an elected body and transfers to the voters the power to decide whether any given individual is elected or not. It is certainly clear that the opposition to PR was not always scrupulous. "In Victoria ... the abolition of the system after a single election in 1921 was due to a campaign against it by a local paper, which spread the false statement that ballots were transferred under PR to persons for whom those who cast them had not voted."

A great deal more evidence is available from the long-continued use of PR/STV in Calgary, Edmonton and Winnipeg, for both city and provincial elections. Winnipeg is of special interest because it changed its electoral system in order to dispel the bitterness left by a general strike in 1919 – a move that was very successful. The premier of Manitoba, distressed by the polarization of Winnipeg between a poverty-stricken north and a relatively wealthy south, persuaded the secretary of the Proportional Representation Society of Canada to supervise a trial of STV in the 1920 provincial election. The whole city voted as one (avoiding drawing attention to its class divisions) to elect ten members, and there were 41 candidates, which meant a long count, spread over several days. Although the electors were facing this task for the first time, they do not seem to have found it formidable; there was a 75 per cent poll and only 1.7 per cent of invalid papers (2.5 in the preceding X-vote election). Nearly all the voters found themselves with a member who was at least of the party they favoured and in most cases was also their first choice among its candidates. Only the backers of the miscellaneous Independents failed to elect their first-preference candidate, and most of their later preferences contributed to the election of a party candidate whom they favoured – usually Liberal or Conservative.

	candidates	votes	seats won
Labour	10	20,167	4
Liberal	10	14,423	4
Conservative	10	6,475	2
Independent	11	6,362	0

Leaders of all three parties expressed satisfaction with the new system. The Attorney-General (Liberal) said, "I have not now and never have had a single regret in the efforts made by me personally in connection with the introduction of this reform.... Everything claimed for it ... was clearly accomplished". WJ Tupper, a Conservative, agreed: "In my opinion the test that proportional representation underwent in this city during the last provincial election was successful." The Labour candidate who headed the poll said that "while it is probable that under the old system ... Labour would have secured more seats, the party does not desire to increase its representation by taking advantage of an antiquated system of election. Winnipeg's experience certainly demonstrates the superiority of PR". In a later election, a candidate said he was "amazed that so many people seemed to understand it. People had fun numbering the candidates" and found the count exciting.

A very detailed analysis of Winnipeg's 1945 election for its ten members of the provincial legislature was carried out by John Fitzgerald, of the British PR Society. Most voters supported one of the parties by voting 1, 2, 3 ... for its candidates, and large numbers went on to candidates bearing some relation to that party (e.g. from Coalition Liberal to Coalition Conservative); this of course produced proportional representation of the parties and other groups. The voters showed very clearly their opinion of the candidates personally; for instance the first-preference votes for the CCF (Co-operative Commonwealth Federation) candidates were:

Farmer	11,237	elected first
Stinson	7,773	elected fourth
Gray	4,975	elected fifth
Swales	2,662	elected seventh
Stapleton	2,329	
Robertson	1,796	

The personal reputation of the one Independent, Stubbs, caused him to be elected with the third largest number of first preferences, 8,309, exceeding the quota of 7,222. The weight given to personality showed itself in a particularly interesting way in the case of the two Communist candidates, Kardash and Zuken, one of whom was elected ninth. That party has a reputation for iron discipline, but by no means all of those two candidates' supporters followed the party line. When Zuken was eliminated, most of his votes did indeed go to Kardash, but one third of them went to candidates of other parties. On the other hand Kardash was evidently well thought of personally by many people who did not share his political views, for he picked up by transfer from candidates of other parties enough votes to secure his eventual election. Besides this lone Communist and the Independent, three parties secured representation, each in exact proportion to its first-preference votes and by its most popular candidate(s).

As in New York, the election of this one Communist was used in an attempt to discredit the system on the ground that it favours extremists. The City Clerk of Winnipeg, in a letter dated 26 January 1962 and referring to the latest city council election, said that

The charge that PR favours the Communists is viciously untrue. The truth is that PR favours no one but gives each party or group representation in accordance with its voting strength. Because it does this the Communists get representation in accordance with their voting strength, as do Liberals, Conservatives and Socialists. Just how this is "favouring" Communists any more than it is "favouring" the other political parties escapes me. What PR does is to prevent a group representing a bare majority or even a minority from gaining a monopoly of representation.

How it does this was strikingly illustrated in the Alberta provincial election of 1948, when Social Credit (including one Independent Social Credit) did achieve, with 58 per cent of the votes cast, a complete monopoly of all the seats *except* the ten filled by STV in Calgary and Edmonton.

RURAL AREAS (single-member constituencies, alternative vote)

	Social Credit	CCF	Liberal	others
votes	122,665	43,127	39,046	6,891
seats	46	0	0	1 (Ind.SC)

CALGARY AND EDMONTON (each a 5-seat constituency, using STV)

	Social Credit	CCF	Liberal	others
votes	25,147	13,260	16,695	13,769
seats	5	2	2	1

Calgary adopted STV as long ago as 1916 and its experience led Edmonton to follow suit in 1922. One immediate effect in Calgary was to treble the turnout within those six years. (It is a general experience that when electors know that their vote is almost certain to affect the result in the way they wish, they are much more inclined to use it.) Edmonton illustrates also both the possibility, under STV, of special provisions to meet special needs and the fact that such provisions are seldom necessary. The normal counting rules were modified so as to ensure that the south side of the city should always have a number of aldermen at least in proportion to its population and in any case not fewer than three. In the first STV election this operated to give South Side one more alderman than it would other-wise have had, but in the second and third elections it got its proportional number without the aid of this special rule. Fair representation of geographical areas within a constituency is usually obtained by the natural tendency of voters to give preference, other things being equal, to candidates from their own locality.

Later developments in Manitoba not only illustrate the effects of different systems on the result of an election but also give some indication of public opinion on the subject. An Act of the provincial parliament in 1957 did away with PR in Winnipeg (which was first one 10-member constituency and later three, returning four members

Table 2 *Manitoba Provincial Elections*

		1953					1959			
		LP	PC	CCF	SC	OTHERS	LP	PC	CCF	OTHERS
WINNIPEG STV in three 4-member constituencies										
CENTRE	votes, %	27.4	12.5	26.9	6.8	26.4	converted to 13 single-member constituencies			
	seats won	1	1	1	–	1				
	seats in pr. to votes	1	1	1	–	1				
NORTH	votes, %	42.5	9.0	43.2	4.6	0.7				
	seats won	2	–	2	–	–				
	seats in pr. to votes	2	–	2	–	–				
SOUTH	votes, %	33.7	41.5	20.8	4.0	–				
	seats won	1	2	1	–	–				
	seats in pr. to votes	1	2	1	–	–				
CITY TOTAL	votes, %	34.1	23.6	29.0	5.4	8.6	20.6	45.3	32.8	1.3
	seats won	4	3	4	–	1	0	8	5	0
	seats in pr. to votes	4	3	4	–	1	3	6	4	0
REMAINDER OF PROVINCE	votes, %	27.9	30.5	14.0	19.4	8.2	34.7	46.6	17.9	0.8
	seats won	28*	9	1	2	4	11	28	5	–
	seats in pr. to votes	12	14	6	8	4	15	21	8	–
TOTALS FOR MANITOBA	votes, %	29.8	28.5	18.3	15.2	8.2	30.6	46.3	22.2	0.9
	seats won	32*	12	5	2	5	11	36	10	–
	seats in pr. to votes	17	16	10	9	4	18	27	12	–

*plus 1 unopposed

each), dividing it into single-member constituencies like the rest of the province. The results of the elections immediately before and after this are shown in Table 2 (p 121). Within Winnipeg, the largest party (Liberal) lost one third of its votes but *all* of its four seats, leaving only two parties, of which the larger (Conservative) got an 8 to 5 majority of the seats for only 45.3 per cent of the total votes. Moreover, although the other party, CCF, did win five seats, it lost that of the member whom the voters had shown to be by far the most popular of its three candidates in the former 4-member constituency of Winnipeg Centre. If the motive of the government party for making the change was that it disliked having its 67 per cent of the rural seats reduced to 59 per cent by the Winnipeg members elected under PR, its punishment was swift and severe. In the 1959 election it actually gained fractionally in votes over the whole province (30.6 per cent compared with 29.8) but lost two thirds of its seats! From having a comfortable overall majority it was reduced to only 11 seats against 36 for the Conservatives and 10 for the CCF.

The change in system was imposed by the provincial legislature, in which Winnipeg members were heavily outnumbered, and there is nothing to show that it was desired by the people most affected, i.e. the Winnipeg electors who alone had had any experience of PR. Such evidence as the 1959 election gives is to the contrary. In the province outside Winnipeg, that is in the part not affected by the 1957 Act, the vote for the government responsible for that Act rose from 27.0 to 34.7 per cent, but in Winnipeg, whose electors had seen their fair electoral system destroyed by that government, its vote fell from 34.1 to 20.6 per cent.

In 1976 the Manitoba Law Reform Commission recommended that the province return to the alternative vote for the rural areas and STV for the city, but this advice appears to have been ignored.

All this experience of the single transferable vote, in Scotland and overseas, shows that it is a perfectly practicable method of electing local councils, well within the comprehension of the voters, reflecting their support for the parties but reflecting equally the views of those who think party should be subordinated to local considerations and to the fitness of individual candidates for council service. What prospect is there of its being extended to British local authorities?

At the time of writing, another in the series of private members' bills is being promoted, to give councils power to change to STV if they wish. In the meantime, there has been a step actually taken by one council which is likely to be copied by others. Medina borough council, on the Isle of Wight, invited a representative of the Electoral Reform Society to demonstrate by a mock election the use of STV by the council to elect its committees. The council subsequently amended its standing orders to provide for the use of STV in all its internal elections from 14 May 1981. Also, a private bill is being promoted to give the island a single unitary authority in place of the three which that small area now has (county and two districts). This bill includes provision for the new authority to be elected by STV.

Devolution

In 1969 a Royal Commission on the Constitution (the Kilbrandon Commission) was set up "to examine the present functions of the central legislature and government in relation to the several countries, nations and regions of the United Kingdom" and to consider what changes might be desirable. Its voluminous report,* published in 1973, covers a wide field and is associated particularly with proposals for a measure of self-government in Scotland and Wales. Members of the Commission held divergent views on many matters but came to just one unanimous conclusion:

> The Scottish or Welsh assembly would be a single-chamber body of about 100 members, directly elected for a fixed term of four years by the single transferable vote form of proportional representation.

The Commission stressed that this recommendation was not a general one but related to regional assemblies only, where the possible desirability of a working majority for one party did not apply. "It would be no bad thing for a regional government to have to pay regard ... to the views of minority parties, or indeed to be obliged to seek a consensus with them."

The report's discussions on the relative merits of different electoral systems remains of lasting value and the subject got a good airing in both houses of parliament, but the practical outcome has so far been nil. To begin with the government, in its white paper, *Democracy and Devolution: Proposals for Scotland and Wales* (September 1974) chose to reject the one unanimous recommenda-

---

* HM Stationery Office, 2 vols, Cmnd. 5460, 5460-1, October 1973.

tion of the Commission and proposed that membership of the assemblies "will be on the same system as membership of the United Kingdom parliament, i.e. a single member elected from a geographical area". To make matters worse, it was proposed in the first election to elect *two* members from each of the existing Westminster constituencies, thus making almost certain the kind of result that was common in our former 2-member constituencies, exemplified by Stockport in 1945

Conservative	31,039	elected
Conservative	30,792	elected
Labour	29,674	
Labour	29,630	
Liberal	14,994	
Liberal	14,942	

and doubling the injustice. The reason for this was simply speed: those constituencies were later to be divided into single-member ones but this would take a boundary commission quite a long time. Had the Kilbrandon proposal been accepted, no such expedient would have been necessary, for existing natural units such as cities or counties would simply have elected by STV a number of members proportional to their electorate, with no new boundaries needing to be drawn. The Electoral Reform Society had a schedule already prepared.*

Parliamentary debates on these proposals did at least produce considerable discussion of electoral systems, and although members of both houses still in many cases showed themselves to be very ill-informed, support for a proportional system of some kind rose steadily from 62 members of all parties in the first division to 162 in the last.

Eventually the whole devolution project fell through, for parliament decided to submit the government's proposals to referendum, with the remarkable provision that they must be accepted by at least 40 per cent of the entire electorate. An odd proposal to come from a government claiming a "mandate" on the ground of votes for it amounting to only 29 per cent of the electorate! To nobody's surprise, that 40 per cent was not reached, and indeed in Wales devolution

---

* *Electing the Scottish Assembly*, James Gilmour and James Woodward-Nutt.

as embodied in the government's bill was rejected by a large majority; in Scotland there was a "yes" majority amounting to 51.6 per cent of those voting but only 32.9 per cent of those entitled to vote. Devolution has, for the present, ceased to be a live issue.

7

Global Village

At the other end of the spectrum from the parish council are the increasingly numerous international organizations which seek some involvement of individuals in their government. Their elections are bound to involve a number of different interests which cut across, and may conflict with, one another. A voter will most likely wish to have a representative of his own nation, or at least his own continent, but he will also wish to elect someone whose views on how the organization should be run are similar to his own. An English voter will not consider himself properly represented by an Englishman of quite different views. It is also highly desirable for the development of a corporate spirit that voters should be encouraged to consider the merits and defects of all candidates, not only of those sharing their own nationality or other special interest. For such elections, anything that confines the voter within a party structure is unsuitable and the case for the flexible single transferable vote is overwhelming.

In the United Nations and similar organizations votes are cast by appointed delegates on behalf of their nations, but there now exists one body, the European parliament, whose members are elected directly by the same people who elect the ten national parliaments (plus or minus a few special cases such as British peers). This has not yet become a truly international election, since voting takes place within each member state separately, for candidates belonging to that state. However, those limitations have already been breached to the extent that, for instance, in the 1979 election the Irish Republic and the Netherlands accepted votes from all EEC nationals living in their territories and a number of leading politicians spoke in other countries on behalf of candidates in kindred parties.

The Treaty of Rome requires a scheme to be drawn up for elections to its parliament by a common system in all member states, but no agreement on a common system was achieved by the first election in 1979 and there seems little prospect of it for the second in 1984. Therefore in 1979 each member state used its own system, which was generally the same as that for its national parliament or nearly so. The main exception was France, which used ordered party lists in the whole country as one constituency; also the Federal Republic of Germany used party lists only, without the first vote in single-member constituencies. Although no two of the nine states used identical systems, seven were very similar with their party list PR systems, Ireland of course used the single transferable vote, and the United Kingdom was the odd man out with its first past the post in single-member constituencies – except in Northern Ireland. The history of this exception is interesting. When a meeting of ministers finally agreed on the numbers of seats for each member state, the British prime minister welcomed the rise from 80 to 81 for each of the four largest states, because that would enable Northern Ireland to have three seats, two for the two-thirds Protestant majority and one for the one-third Catholic minority. But, objected the German foreign minister, under the British X-vote that could not happen; the majority was bound to take all three seats. There is indeed no way in which boundaries of three single-member constituencies could be drawn so as to give a Catholic majority in any one of them. This had to be admitted and, to avoid flagrant injustice intensifying civil strife, Northern Ireland was allowed to use STV as in all its other elections since 1973, except those for Westminster MPs.

The different system in Britain led to very different results. First, preparation for the poll took far longer, the boundary commission having to do a great deal of work and its recommendations being subjected to much criticism. It was instructed to combine the 623 constituencies of mainland Britain so as to produce 78 Euro-constituencies having electorates as nearly as possible equal, and this it did very successfully. This, however, could be achieved only by disregarding, in many cases, obvious natural boundaries. England had to return 66 MEPs, giving an average electorate for each of 516,436. The county of Lincolnshire, with its seven Westminster constituencies, had an electorate of 477,794, near enough to the average for that county to be taken as one Euro-constituency. But Devon had well over the average, 695,716, while Cornwall was much below the average, with 310,489 electors. So Plymouth had to be detached from its county and added to Cornwall, which did not please the local people at all. The worst fate befell the county of Wiltshire, which lost its identity altogether, being divided among four of its neighbouring counties. Under any proportional system (which necessarily involves multi-member constituencies) this would have been avoided. For instance, the European Assembly Elections bill as originally presented to the House of Commons provided for a regional list system* under which the whole of Wiltshire would have been incorporated in a 6-member constituency of South West England. Besides irritating local patriots and making it difficult for people to identify with their Euro-constituency, the boundaries of single-member constituencies could not avoid, in many cases, favouring one party or another. This is seen most clearly in Greater London, where different ways of combining its 92 Westminster constituencies into 10 European ones could give the Labour party anything from five to none of the ten seats for the same votes as it had polled in the preceding Greater London Council election.† With PR, London could be one 10-member constituency or one 6- and one 4-member constituency divided by the natural boundary of the Thames, and either way the parties would get their fair share of the seats – with somewhat more accuracy under the 10-member scheme.

All the work devoted to producing equality between electorates did nothing whatsoever to produce equality in the effects of different people's votes. Of those who voted Conservative, nearly nine out of every ten got an MEP they had voted for; of those who voted Labour, less than three in ten did, and of those who voted Liberal, none.

Of all the valid votes cast, nearly half (47.6 per cent) were cast for losing candidates and so had no effect on the result. In many places the outcome was a foregone conclusion – few people can have expected that a non-Conservative vote in West Sussex or a non-Labour vote in South East Wales would elect anybody – and this must be one reason why the British poll, 32 per cent, was much the lowest in the Community. With so many votes having no effect, it is not surprising that the seats won by the parties bore little relation to their popular support. The Conservatives, with 50.6 per cent of the votes, won 60 out of the 78 seats; Labour, with one third of the votes, got one quarter of the seats, and the largest Liberal

---

* Voting for 1 of 3 to 14 candidates in a party list. Seats proportional to party's total votes, filled by candidates with most votes.

† See EM Syddique, *Representation* No 70, p 4 and RJ Johnson; ibid, No 72, p 23.

party in Europe got no representation at all. The British Conservatives polled half as many votes as the West German Christian Democrats but won 60 seats to the latter's 42; British Labour, with more votes than French Communists, won fewer seats, and the British Liberals, with 13 per cent of the votes and no seats, had more popular support than any of the 17 continental parties that got from one to five seats each.

If these distortions affected only the British, it would be this country's business only, but of course they do not. They upset the balance of the whole parliament, and the other member states are justifiably annoyed. Although the British Conservatives failed to find any continental party with which they could form a group, except for three Danish Conservatives, they form easily the third largest group in the parliament instead of being, in accordance with their votes, on a level with the Communists and the Liberals. The Socialist group consider themselves to have been robbed of eight seats, and the Liberals, deprived of what should have been substantial British support in the actual parliament, have made the Liberal member of the former nominated assembly, Russell Johnston, a kind of honorary member available for consultation.

Thus, all the other EEC members will be ranged against Britain in seeking a proportional system for the whole Community. However, to all of them except Ireland this means a system based on voting for party lists, and this is not really appropriate. European elections should be about European questions – such as for example whether the Community should develop into a true federation or remain something like de Gaulle's "Europe des Patries" – but opinion on such matters often cuts right across the national party lines and cannot be reflected adequately by voting for a party. This was obvious in the British election, where Labour candidates ranged from enthusiastic supporters of the Community to people who would like to take Britain out of it and any Labour supporter who wished to maintain his usual party allegiance could only vote for the one or the other according to where he lived. Similar anomalies appeared in those countries voting for ordered party lists. In France, some on President Giscard's list declared that they would sit with the Liberal group, others with the Christian Democrats, but no voter supporting that list had any means of choosing between them. Belgium, Luxembourg, the Netherlands and Italy all gave some choice between individual candidates but this choice was subsidiary to the party vote. The regional list system suggested by the British

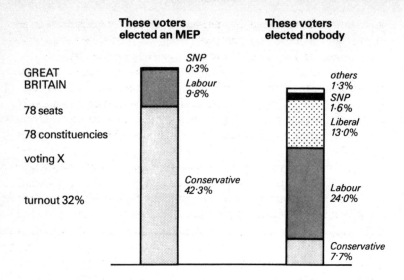

These voters elected an MEP

These voters elected nobody

GREAT BRITAIN

78 seats

78 constituencies

voting X

turnout 32%

SNP 0·3%
Labour 9·8%
Conservative 42·3%

others 1·3%
SNP 1·6%
Liberal 13·0%
Labour 24·0%
Conservative 7·7%

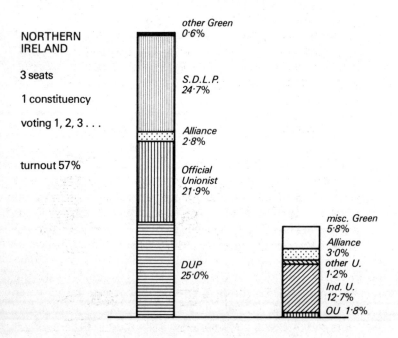

NORTHERN IRELAND

3 seats

1 constituency

voting 1, 2, 3 . . .

turnout 57%

other Green 0·6%
S.D.L.P. 24·7%
Alliance 2·8%
Official Unionist 21·9%
DUP 25·0%

misc. Green 5·8%
Alliance 3·0%
other U. 1·2%
Ind. U. 12·7%
OU 1·8%

Figure 18 European Parliament Election 1979, United Kingdom government but rejected by parliament would have given a large element of choice within any party. Only the Irish, however, were free to vote on European lines to any extent they wished.

This included the people of Northern Ireland, whose behaviour presents a great contrast with the rest of the United Kingdom. Instead of being limited to one candidate from each of (usually) three or four parties, they had a free choice (with no risk of "splitting the vote") among thirteen candidates, representing different shades of Orange and Green as well as different opinions about Europe. They also knew that the choice they expressed would most likely affect the result (a 3 to 1 chance, compared with 1 to 1 in Britain); doubtless this contributed to the relatively high poll, 57 per cent compared with Britain's 32 per cent. Not only did three quarters of the voters actually contribute to the election of a candidate whom they supported; the other quarter also had one among the three elected candidates who was of the same general complexion as their first choice. The known personal popularity of Ian Paisley among the Protestant community was confirmed by his immediate election with a substantial surplus of first-preference votes; the most popular Catholic candidate, John Hume, was an easy second. Most, though by no means all, of Paisley's surplus went to other Protestant Unionist candidates and secured the election of one of them. This, however, was not the leader of another Unionist party but his rival. Supporters of the Official Unionist party had a choice of two

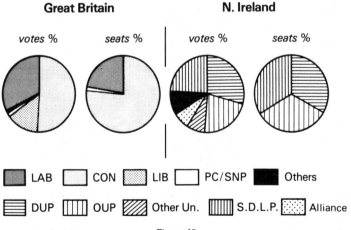

Figure 19

candidates, West (its leader) and Taylor. Not only did the latter lead already on first preferences, he also received by transfer more than three times as many votes as West did before his elimination. Clearly, Taylor is more generally welcome as a representative than West would have been.

The Republic of Ireland voted in four constituencies, based on the historic provinces and each returning three, four or five members. There has been some criticism of the results on the ground that the Labour party is over-represented, the national totals being:

	first pref	*votes*	*seats won*
Fianna Fáil	464,451	34.68%	5
Fine Gael	443,652	33.13%	4
Labour	193,898	14.48%	4
Sinn Féin the Workers' Party	43,942	3.28%	—
Community Democrats of Ireland	3,630	0.27%	—
Independent	189,499	14.15%	2
totals	1,339,072	99.99%	15

The main reason for the anomaly is the small constituencies, half of them returning only three members each. In one of these, Leinster, the first-preference votes were:

Fianna Fáil	127,327
Fine Gael	125,021
Labour	40,072
SFWP	14,476

The quota being 76,725, clearly each of the two largest parties must win one seat; who gets the third seat? If these votes had been for party lists, the d'Hondt rule would have given it to Fianna Fáil, but twice as many seats for it as for the nearly equal Fine Gael does not look any more satisfactory than the actual 1 : 1 : 1 result. What the single transferable vote did was to let the voters decide between those two possibilities. They quite plainly chose to give Labour that third seat, for its one candidate received by transfer from other parties' candidates a total of 18,504 votes compared with 9,624 and 2,792 for FF and FG respectively. The three-party representation does appear to have given the most general satisfaction that is possible with that small number of seats.

Had the whole country been one 15-member constituency, a much larger number of voters would have been represented by their first-preference candidate and (assuming most people do vote on party lines) FF and FG, each with over five times the quota of 83,693, would have won five seats each, Labour two and Independents two, leaving only one seat in doubt.

A feature of the election was the success of the two Independents, who were the only candidates to obtain a large surplus of first-preference votes.

8

Women and Blacks

When women are classed with ethnic minorities as people too seldom found in parliaments or in other influential positions, they often feel insulted – not because of any racial prejudice on their part but because they are not a minority. More than half the British electorate is female, yet there are only 19 women MPs to 616 men and there have never been more than 29 (in 1964) to 601 men (4.6 per cent).

Is Britain unique in this respect? By no means; it is not even the worst country in respect of women in its legislature. Our 3.0 per cent of women MPs compares with 4 per cent in the USA, 5 in Canada and New Zealand, 3 in India, 5 in France and 2 per cent in Australia. On the other hand, all the other European democracies are well ahead even of the 4.6 per cent which is Britain's best so far. Finland tops the list, with 23.5 per cent women, closely followed by Norway and Sweden, with 4 others over 10 per cent (including Switzerland where women were enfranchised only in 1971) and another four with between two and three times the British figure.

	% women in parliament		*% women in parliament*
France	5	Sweden	21
New Zealand	5	Denmark	17
Australia, Ho Reps.	2	Australia, Senate	15
W Germany, 1st votes	4	W Germany, 2nd votes	12
USA	4	Switzerland	11
Canada	4	Italy	8
United Kingdom	3	Irish Republic	7
India	3	Israel	6
Finland	24	Greece	4
Norway	23		

Is there any common factor shared on the one hand by all the countries with very low female representation and on the other hand by those with higher figures? Yes. All of the former elect their parliaments from single-member constituencies; all of the latter have proportional systems – which necessarily involve multi-member constituencies. Moreover, there is one country which supplies a contrast within itself: West Germany, which elects half the Bundestag exactly like the House of Commons and the other half by voting for party lists in constituencies (the Länder) each electing up to 75 members. This second half always contains several times as many women as the first. In the 1976 election the percentages were respectively 12.9 and 2.8; in 1980, 12.4 and 4.4. Another contrast within one country is in Australia, where the same people, voting at the same time, produced by the alternative vote 2.4 per cent of women in the House of Representatives but, by PR/STV, 14.7 per cent of women in the Senate.

The whole series of Australian federal and state elections leaves no room for doubt that a woman's chance of election is much greater in a multi-member constituency. In the table below, the most significant figures are those for the larger assemblies; in the small ones (Tasmania and South Australia's upper house) the addition or subtraction of just one woman has an exaggerated effect.

WOMEN IN AUSTRALIAN LEGISLATURES

	lower house				upper house			
	AV		PR		AV		PR	
	number	%	number	%	number	%	number	%
Federal parliament	3	2.4					10	14.7
New South Wales	1	1.0					7	11.7
Victoria	3	3.7			2	5.6		
Queensland	2	2.4						
South Australia	1	2.1					2	10.0*
Western Australia	1	1.8			3	9.4		
Tasmania			2	5.7	1	5.3		

* party list

A change with time inside one country is to be seen in France. Women were enfranchised there in 1945 and made a promising start with 7 per cent of the elected members. However, far from any improvement on this, there has been a steady decline. Partly this is a natural consequence of fading war-time memories, heroines of the Resistance having retired and not been replaced, but the trend has certainly been reinforced by the change in 1958 from multi-member to single-member constituencies. In the 1975 election the figure was down to 1.7 per cent and an agitation for more representation succeeded in raising this in the next election only to 3 per cent, while in the election to the European parliament, under party list PR, it was 22.2 per cent.

Why should the multi-member constituency tend to increase the number of women elected? Simply because it greatly reduces the obstacle they have to surmount in order to become candidates. To have any chance of election, it is almost everywhere essential to be chosen as its candidate by one of the major parties, and each party has some form of selection committee for this purpose. Under the British system, first past the post in single-member constituencies, a party is forced to select just one candidate; to have more would split its vote and in most cases ensure defeat. (Under the alternative vote, as in Australia, it could have a second candidate without this risk but this does not happen in practice; rival candidates of the same party would advertise disunity and the parties avoid it.) A party must choose its one candidate so as to attract as many voters as possible and repel as few as possible. It may be prejudiced against women in parliament, but even if it is not it probably believes that the electors are – that a woman will attract fewer votes than a man. There is very little evidence to support this, but the belief is what matters. "Of course there ought to be more women candidates, but she wouldn't go down *here*." In a multi-member constituency, on the contrary, the pressure is in the reverse direction. Any party large enough to have hopes of winning more than one seat must select more than one candidate, and it is in the party's interest to select them so as to make the widest possible appeal to the voters – including both men and women, as well as any "wings" there may be within the party. Also, if the system is one of ordered party lists, the party will usually wish to avoid advertising prejudice by putting all its women low on the list.

Within the two groups of countries there are wide variations, depending on the social climate, and it is no surprise to find Italy far below Finland. Nowhere has the female half of the population attained half the seats, nor does this seem likely in the foreseeable future. It is more difficult for a mother than for a father to combine family responsibilities with being an MP, and there are still fewer women than men with parliamentary ambitions, but in so far as women are able and willing to pursue that career a proportional electoral system opens doors to them. If the system is one of party lists, the extent of that opening depends on influencing the party organizations. They are in any case unlikely to advertise blatant prejudice by giving men all the top places, but some pressure for a fair share of them is found necessary. This is of course easier where the voters have a choice between candidates and can give preference to a woman if they wish. That is the case, for example, in Belgium. In their 1974 election a women's list got few votes and no seats but personal votes for women among the established parties' candidates increased greatly, contributing directly to a rise in the number elected (from 12 to 21 out of the 318 directly elected members of both houses) and encouraging the parties to treat them with greater respect. In elections to the German Bundestag no such choice exists, but it would appear from the 1980 election (see page 135) that the parties, having got used to the presence of women elected from the Land lists, are becoming more willing to select one as their sole candidate in a single-member constituency.

In Ireland, under STV, the decision as to which sex is elected lies entirely with the voters, who can always overrule a party choice if they feel strongly about it, and it seems at first sight disappointing that there are so few women in the Dáil. However, that is only a fair reflection of Irish society, in which, with a few outstanding exceptions, women have been accustomed to take a back seat in public life. They have now begun to assert themselves, and the electoral system enables them to do so effectively. This first became apparent in the 1977 general election, notably in Cork City, where a woman Independent candidate waged a vigorous campaign involving the serious grievance of a local woman. She was not elected, but, like others in a similar position, polled much better than most people expected, and there was much favourable comment on the quality of the women candidates. It was clear that many electors had begun to use their preferences for the express purpose of electing women. In the four constituencies where there were two women candidates (in each case of different parties), when one of them was eliminated, the transfers went as follows:

	to a woman	to a man of this woman's party
Cork City	335	211
Dublin Rathmines	55	6
Dublin South East	112	54 and 48
Roscommon-Leitrim	169	58 and 42

In Roscommon-Leitrim the woman getting the 169 votes was a sitting Deputy, much better known than either of her male colleagues, but in Cork the opposite was the case.

This tendency was more conspicuous in the local government elections of 1979, and in the elections the same day to the European parliament. An article by Christina Murphy in the *Irish Times* of 15 June 1979 gives a long list of spectacular successes by women in both elections. In Waterford, for instance, the previously unknown Katherine Bulbulia not only became the first woman on the county council but also topped the poll, ahead of a front-bench Deputy of her own party. A number of councils now have 20 to 25 per cent of women, and there are two out of the 15 European MPs. In the 1981 election to the Dáil there was much less evidence of voting for women as such but more won seats on their merits, regardless of sex. The total number of women in the Dáil rose from 6 out of 148 (4.1 per cent) to 11 out of 166 (6.6 per cent) and included two prominent feminists. One woman was Minister of Health and Social Welfare in the new government. The trend is expected to continue, but it is entirely in the hands of the voters.

COLOUR BAR

If women find it difficult to persuade any party to select one of them as its only candidate, much more so do coloured people. They have begun to appear in local councils, but there are still none in the House of Commons. "Of course blacks ought to have a voice in parliament, but we daren't adopt one here; we'd lose too many white votes." But no reasonable white could object to having one black candidate among three (and the unreasonable ones would probably be outweighed by blacks attracted to that ticket), so there was no bar to the selection of Dr David Pitt by the Labour party as one of its three candidates for Stoke Newington and Hackney North in the London County Council election of 1961. He quickly proved his value on the council and started on the career which led to his peerage.

The 3-member division thus facilitated the acceptance of a black candidate, but X-voting meant that he was elected simply because his party was well ahead of any other; the voters could neither promote his election nor prevent it without deserting their party. With the single transferable vote of course they could.

The need for people to be able to elect a representative of their own ethnic group or religion is easily recognized where bodies governing education are concerned. The success of STV in representing the different religious communities on the Scottish education authorities has been discussed on pages 105–6; for the same reasons it was introduced in 1970 for the New York school boards. The ethnic minorities there involved were mainly black and Puerto Rican, with some Chinese. In 1970 the black and Puerto Rican populations of New York City exceeded 10 and 17 per cent respectively but the 37-member city council contained only 2 blacks and no Puerto Ricans. But in the STV elections for the school boards that same year those two ethnic groups obtained seats in almost exact proportion to their numbers.

If a voter attaches overwhelming importance to being represented by someone of his own ethnic group, he will vote 1, 2, 3, etc. for all candidates of that group, beginning, no doubt, with those of the party he most favours, but including those of other parties. Studies of New York city council elections (by STV from 1937 to 1947) have shown very few people going to those lengths,* but the ethnic groups do nevertheless obtain nearly their proportional share of the seats because it is the first preferences which are by far the most important. A black elector who votes 1 for a black Democrat and 2 for a white Democrat is likely to contribute to the representation both of his party and of his ethnic community.

This is of great importance for the peaceful development of countries where racial divisions are acute. In former colonies attaining independence, it has usually been thought essential to provide in the constitution for fair representation of the main racial (or perhaps religious) groups, but too often this has been done by instituting separate electoral rolls, so that for example whites hold

* See Belle Zeller and Hugh A Bone, *American Political Science Review*, December 1948, p 1140, and authorities quoted therein.

one election for white candidates and blacks a separate one for black candidates. This has the great disadvantage of emphasizing the difference between them (and, if a majority system of election is used, of exaggerating it), discouraging voters from considering the merits of candidates in the other group and hampering the development of political parties across the racial divisions. With the single transferable vote form of PR there is no need for separate rolls; all can vote together to elect representatives of all races. This is true even if one race constitutes quite a small minority – as whites do in an overwhelmingly black African state. If some group is too small to poll one quota of votes in any constituency but it is nevertheless felt that it must have a voice in the elected body, this can easily be secured by a simple modification of the normal rules: if the last candidate of that group is at the bottom of the poll, he is not eliminated but is declared elected, the rest of the count proceeding normally.

In the first such election it is likely that voting will be largely on racial lines, but the voter must discriminate among the various candidates of his own race – on account of their party or anything else he considers important – and he is encouraged to go on to candidates of other races with whom he feels some agreement. As time goes on and the races get accustomed to working together, party or other considerations may tend to assume more importance than race, and candidates who have earned a good reputation will find themselves being elected with the help of votes from other races. The special rule for representation of a very small minority may even become redundant.

It is the general experience that STV does, in fact, have such reconciling effects, but it has not yet been tested in less developed countries where illiteracy may present a problem. The nearest approach to this has been in Malta, where at the time when STV was introduced about half the electors in some constituencies were illiterate. It was found possible to cope with this by letting the voter give his choice verbally to the presiding officer in secrecy, which is quite acceptable if those conducting the election are fully trusted. There could, however, be means devised for the illiterate to mark his own paper. The use of symbols for parties (e.g. the familiar hammer and sickle) is found even in Europe, in Italy and Greece, and it might be extended to candidates, those of one party being represented perhaps by different animals, those of another by different plants, and so on. Even a voter knowing no means of indicating preferences should have no great difficulty in putting some kind of mark beside the symbol of the one candidate he most wants, and since first preferences are much the most important this would give a reasonably proportional result. Those who could write numbers would be allowed and encouraged to do so and their votes would be more certain to be effective – the literate would have some advantage over the illiterate which might be no bad thing. Another possibility is to allow the candidate for whom the illiterate has voted to decide whom that vote shall be transferred to if the need arises.

Use of the single transferable vote in such circumstances would put a different complexion on the case for a one-party state. In European democracies that evokes a picture of a dictatorship suppressing more or less brutally all opinions but one. An African, on the other hand, will very likely support it on the ground that he dislikes the idea of an opposition party whose business it is to oppose. And isn't he right? Certainly a government should be opposed by those who think it to be acting wrongly, but no government is wrong all the time. We should not have let ourselves be led into the practice of opposing everything just because it emanates from the government party (or of supporting it for the same reason). Government proposals should be supported or opposed on their merits, not according to their origin, and the opposition may perfectly well come from people in the same party as those giving support. That has indeed been happening to an increasing extent during 1981. We find in Britain that attitudes on certain questions often cut right across the party lines or class divisions.*

STV tends to break down opposition for the sake of opposition. It draws the voter's attention to the differences of opinion that exist within his own party and to points on which he finds agreement with people in other parties, and it undermines the power of a party to make all its MPs vote in the same lobby. The desire to impose a one-party system will therefore be less.

At the same time, if a country does decide to have only one party, this can be perfectly compatible with democracy, for STV will produce, within that party, spokesmen for different shades of opinion. There are actual examples of one-party states where there is lively debate within the party and elections in which the voters

* Paper by Bo Särlvik, Ivor Crewe and David Robertson, University of Essex, April 1981.

often replace a cabinet minister with someone more to their liking (Tanganyika, Zambia, Kenya). However, under their electoral systems, inherited from the British, the happy working of the one party depends greatly on enlightened leaders with democratic instincts. Firmer foundations can be laid by an electoral system that allows the voters to decide whether they think one party sufficient or feel a need for more, and in either case reflects their support for, or opposition to, particular politicians and particular proposals.

The single transferable vote functions equally well, whether separate parties exist or not.

9

Voluntary Organizations

From its conception, and long before any parliament considered being elected by the single transferable vote, that system was used by its pioneers for elections in bodies of which they were members. The election by Rowland Hill's schoolboys has already been described (p 46) and his father, Thomas Wright Hill, also introduced it in 1821 for elections in the Society for Literary and Scientific Improvement. Voting was on signed ballot papers, on which the voter wrote the name of his one preferred candidate. Any candidate whose name appeared on five papers was elected and any surplus papers over the five (selected by lot) were returned to their originators (hence the need for signing them) so that they could add the name of the candidate to which they wished their paper to be transferred. When all surpluses had been dealt with, elimination from the bottom followed. Clearly, this has all the essentials of STV without its later refinements.

This early example illustrates one enormous advantage of STV over all other forms of proportional representation – that it is equally suitable for all kinds of elections; for the committee of a little local society as much as for a parliament. Its function is to express and give effect to the wishes of the voters, and whether those wishes relate to political parties or to anything else matters not at all. A large and rapidly increasing number of voluntary organizations have come to recognize the importance of having all points of view properly represented on their committees and to realize that this is easily ensured. "Supervote" justifies its name by its capacity for universal application.

One of the earliest of the important bodies involved was the Church of England. STV was applied to Church Assembly elections

(House of Laity from 1920, Proctors of the lower houses of Convocation of Canterbury and York from 1921) and then to the General Synod which replaced those bodies in 1970. For the first Synod elections some dioceses were allowed to divide their area into single-member constituencies, using the alternative vote, but a resolution of Synod in 1972 laid down that in future no constituency might return fewer than three members. The effect has been to give fair representation to shades of opinion within the Church, while not causing them to develop into parties organized one against another. In any General Synod election it can be seen that Evangelical and Anglo-Catholic voters respectively usually give preference to candidates of their persuasion; hence those two groups secure representation in proportion to their voting strength.

Equally, so do any other groups. How the voters are enabled to achieve this had been shown in Chapter 3 on pages 48 to 51. Since it happens by the spontaneous choice of the voters, the church is saved from the disruptive effects that might follow if fair representation had to be sought by organization on party lines. Twenty years after the adoption of STV, Prebendary Merritt said*: "I do not know who it was who secured the insertion of this system in the constitution, but I always think his statue should stand in Dean's Yard and be inscribed 'The saviour of the Church of England'."

This opinion has not been universally shared, objections being raised on the ground that either voters or returning officers failed to understand the system, but proposals to substitute the block vote or a modification of this were heavily defeated in 1926 and 1953. One objection, which often crops up where there are only a few voters, is that it is wrong for a very small quota of people to be able to elect a representative. But this is really an objection, not to the system, but to the size of the elected body. If, for example, 88 people elect a committee of 10, it is an inescapable arithmetical fact that representation is at the rate of one member per nine electors. What is achieved by STV is that *every* nine voters elect a representative; with X-voting it is probable that one group of nine would get several representatives and another group of nine none.

Far from being influenced by these objections, the Church has shown its satisfaction with STV by extending its use. This began in 1974, when General Synod standing orders were amended to use STV for the election of its own standing committees and its

---

* *Church Times*, 19 August 1949.

representatives on other bodies. In 1978 it was made clear that Diocesan Synods could do likewise and the movement has now extended down to Parochial Church Councils. Also, in February 1976 the General Synod resolved overwhelmingly (with no one speaking against) "that this Synod believes the time has come for a change in the present parliamentary voting system and urges all political parties to adopt a preferential system of proportional representation as a policy commitment for future public elections".

Another very long-standing user of STV is the Royal Arsenal Co-operative Society. This and the London Co-operative Society cover the capital between them and are very similar except in their elections. In the London, voting by X's, there are bitter faction fights, in which one or other of three groups sweeps the board. In the RACS, voting 1, 2, 3 . . ., elections are peaceful and representation is shared fairly. Usually, the only groups visible to the rest of the world are those shown by the candidates' published descriptions, which include sex, age and place of residence, all of which may influence the voters' choice and consequently the result of the election. In 1976, there was also, exceptionally, an open political division, referred to in the press as one between moderates and extremists. Of the 17 candidates for the 8 seats on the Political Purposes Committee, 12 described themselves as members of the Labour party and one as a Communist; two others were shown by transfers and other information to be of similar views to the latter, and the remaining two gave no indication of which group they favoured. The result was as follows:

	Labour	*Communist*	*others*
candidates	12	3	2
first preference votes	1,941	592	108
seats won	6	2	0

This was reported as a gain of one seat for the "moderates".

It was very noticeable that this political division never threatened to overshadow other considerations. There were within each political group very large differences in support for candidates, and while the second "Communist" owed his election mainly to transfers from his party colleague who was elected on first preferences, he also received substantial transfers from "moderates", especially from candidates living in his district. Voters tend naturally to prefer candidates who live near them and who therefore are probably well known to them personally, and if voting were by X's this would tend to give all, or nearly all, the seats to candidates living in the Woolwich area, where the RACS originated and where it still has the greatest membership. With STV, on the contrary, outlying districts also get their spokesmen, as in that same 1976 election:

	Woolwich	Kent	Wimble-don	Surrey	Syden-ham
candidates	6	7	1	2	1
first preferences	1,154	931	394	215	177
seats won	3	2	1	1	1

The transfers gave less evidence of support for men or women as such, but they did in fact get fair representation: 3 women candidates polled a total of 313 first preference votes and one of them was elected; 16 men polled 2,328 and 7 of them were elected. The 5 candidates with no previous committee experience had a total of 2 votes more than the quota of 294, so if those voters had been concerned above all to get new blood on to the committee they would have elected one member; in fact there was little voting along those lines so no newcomer was elected.

For many years the number of organizations breaking away from the X-vote remained small. Then in 1961 came an event that brought the Electoral Reform Society into the limelight: the High Court case regarding ballot-rigging in the Electrical Trades Union. In addition to its work in advocating STV, the Society had for fifty years been conducting elections for various bodies, including the Mineworkers and the Railwaymen (alternative vote) and the National Union of Teachers (PR/STV) and had won a reputation as a returning officer with no possible motive for falsifying the result to the benefit of any particular candidate, but on the contrary, a strong interest in retaining trust as an impartial returning officer. When the people hitherto controlling the ETU were convicted of fraud, those replacing them handed over the entire control of the Union's large and numerous elections to the Society and the resulting publicity helped ERS to become the natural resort of any organization wanting help with its elections. Sometimes all they required was an impartial returning officer; in other cases advice was sought to improve an unsatisfactory voting system.

One example of the latter was the Institution of Electrical Engineers, whose officers had become concerned about the composition of its committee – tending to be self-perpetuating with little or no representation of the younger members. Following advice to use STV, the first election under it was conspicuously successful in giving fair representation to the generations and to all branches of the profession. Naturally, electrical engineers talked of this to other engineers, with the result that the Institutions of Civil and Mechanical Engineers followed suit.

The General Dental Council has been using STV for many years and in 1979 it was joined by the General Medical Council. This was recommended to hold its elections in each of its four regions (England with the Channel Islands and the Isle of Man, Scotland, Wales and Northern Ireland) as one constituency. The first election in the England and islands constituency is described by David Gullick in *World Medicine*, 22 March 1980. He complains that the voters were inadequately instructed in preparation for the formidable task of choosing among 150 candidates for 39 places; nevertheless the result gave general satisfaction. The only serious complaint was of the low poll – 34.26 per cent compared with 43, 44 and 56 per cent respectively in the three much smaller regions. The relatively high poll in Northern Ireland may be due to the voters being already familiar with STV. There were some "parties" involved, in the shape of lists of candidates sponsored by the British Medical Association (39 candidates!), British Hospital Doctors Federation, Medical Women's Federation, Medical Practitioners Union and Overseas Doctors Association. Presumably these sponsorships must have influenced voters' choices, but only in the last did the transfers show anything like solid "party" voting. There was no sponsorship of geographical lists, but each of the National Health Service regions, except the islands, did get at least 1 representative, through the natural tendency of voters to give preference to local candidates whom they know. Representation of specialities and of different branches of the profession seems to be satisfactory except for the unrepresented junior hospital staff – who do, however, have 3 consultants known to be "closely identified with their cause". Women are well represented, with 4 of their 9 candidates elected, and so are the graduates of non-British universities, with 5 elected. In the next election, the inordinately long list of candidates will probably shrink, since sponsoring organizations will have realized that none of them can hope to take anything like all the seats, and, with David Gullick's article and other help, the voters should be better equipped to make the most of their opportunities.

The list of organizations using the single transferable vote is now a very long one, running literally from A to Z, and the following sample will give an idea of its variety.

PR/STV   Amnesty International
          British Mensa
          Church of England
          General Dental Council
          General Medical Council
          Consumers' Association
          Council of Engineering Institutions
          Institute of Administrative Management
                        Management Services
          Institution of Civil Engineers
                        Electrical Engineers
                        Mechanical Engineers
                        Production Engineers
          National Council for Civil Liberties
          National Federation of Housing Associations
          National Union of Teachers
          Royal Arsenal Co-operative Society
          Royal Institute of British Architects
          Shell International Pension Fund
          Zionist Federation

Alternative vote
          Electrical, Electronic, Telecommunication and Plumbing
                Union
          National Union of Journalists
                        Mineworkers
                        Railwaymen

Among the non-parliamentary uses of STV in Ireland, two deserve special mention.

The first is in the Irish Congress of Trade Unions. This body was formed in 1959, accepting affiliation by unions in the whole island and ending a long division between the Republic and Northern Ireland. For the success of this combination it was clearly necessary to have fair representation both of the many trades involved and of the two parts of Ireland. This was secured by using STV to elect 16 members of the Executive Council, with a limitation to 1 member from any one union (2 for unions with more than 50,000 members). While the resulting fair representation of trades was affected by this

limitation, that of the two parts of Ireland was produced only by
the normal operation of STV, the figures for the first election being

	first preference votes	*seats*
candidates from the Republic	246	13
candidates from N Ireland	60	3

The Congress was inaugurated in the middle of the campaign
against de Valera's move to have the Dáil elected by the British
system* and its very effective intervention was one of the decisive
factors in the defeat of that proposal.

The second important event was an Act of the coalition government in 1977 instituting the election of employees to the boards of
state enterprises (7 of them, covering air, sea, road and rail transport,
peat, electricity, fertilisers and sugar beet). This move originated
with the trade unions, Congress in its 1967 annual conference having
passed a resolution supporting worker participation in principle,
and studies of the practical aspects were carried out by the unions,
the employers and the EEC. Each of the 7 enterprises has a board
of 12 members, of whom under the Act one third must be employees.
These 4 are elected by all workers over 18 and having at least one
year's continuous service, STV being relied upon to produce fair
representation of the various interests involved. How it has done so
can be seen from the first election in Aer Lingus. In the result sheet
on page 150, the first transfer was from Lawton, described as
"Production Dublin" and nominated by a group of five trade unions.
Of his 201 votes, 140 went to Tatten, with the same description and
nominators, and the next largest number, 34, to another "Production
Dublin" man, Whelan, and when Whelan was later eliminated Tatten
got most of his votes, so that group with its 3 candidates and over
one quota of first-preference votes elected one representative. The
largest union, the Federated Workers Union of Ireland, nominated
4 candidates for the 4 vacancies and they polled a total of 2,208
first-preference votes, those of the next largest union, the Irish Avia-
tion Executive Staff Association, getting only 973. Had voting been
by 4 X's, that largest union, supported by a little less than half the
voters, would certainly have taken all 4 seats; as it was, FWUI
elected its 2 most popular candidates, IAESA and the group of 5 (973
and 948 first preferences) electing 1 each. There were 2 women

*See p 90.

RESULT

Total Electorate ... 6530
Total Votes Cast ... 5767 (89%)
Invalid Votes ... 31
Total Valid Poll ... 5736
Quota ... 1,148

Candidates Elected — Count
1. JOHN TATTEN — 6TH
2. PAUL BOUSHELL — 8TH
3. KAY GARVEY — 8TH
4. MICHAEL COSTELLO — 10TH

Worker Participation (State Enterprises) Act, 1977

Nominated By	Names of Candidates	First Count Votes	2nd: Tr. of LAYTON's Votes	2nd Result	3rd: Tr. of LAWLOR's Votes	3rd Result	4th: Tr. of CONLAN's Votes	4th Result	5th: Tr. of WHELAN's Votes	5th Result	6th: Tr. of SHERIDAN's Votes	6th Result	7th: Tr. of CROGHAN's Votes	7th Result	8th: Tr. of WALSH's Votes	8th Result	9th: Tr. of BOUSHELL's Surplus	9th Result	10th: Tr. of GARVEY's Surplus	10th Result	11th Tr.	11th Result
FWUI	BOUSHELL Paul	732	+4	736	+69	805	+24	829	+74	903	+24	927	+28	955	+457	1,414	-266	1,148	—	1,148		1,148
ITGWU	CONLAN Pat	234	—	234	+6	240	-240															
IAESA	COSTELLO Michael	563	+4	567	+5	572	+34	606	+7	613	+74	687	+111	798	+51	849	+121	970	+38	1,008		1,008
IALPA	CROGHAN Barney	465	+5	470	+3	473	+25	498	+5	503	+88	591	-591									
FWUI	GARVEY Kay	642	+6	648	+28	676	+13	689	+22	711	+27	738	+293	1,031	+190	1,221	—	1,221	-73	1,148		1,148
ITGWU	GRIFFIN Eamon	545	+3	548	+44	592	+78	670	+14	684	+80	764	+15	779	+26	805	+145	950	+35	985		985
FWUI	LAWLOR Billy	204	—	204	-204																	
NUSMWI, AGEMOU, AUEW, EETPU, NEETU	LAYTON Alfie	201	-201																			
IAESA	SHERIDAN Jim	410	—	410	+5	415	+9	424	+2	426	-426											
NEETU, AGEMOU, AUEW, EETPU, NUSMWI	TATTEN John	747	+140	887	+6	893	+13	906	+230	1,136	+17	1,153	—	1,153	—	1,153	—	1,153	—	1,153		1,153
FWUI	WALSH Josephine	630	+2	632	+29	661	+22	683	+33	716	+30	746	+23	769	-769							
ETU	WHELAN Eddie	363	+34	397	+3	400	+4	404	-404													
	Non Transferable Papers not effective		3	3	+6	9	+18	27	+17	44	+86	130	+121	251	+43	294	—	294	—	294		294
	TOTAL	5,736		5,736		5,736		5,736		5,736		5,736		5,736		5,736		5,736		5,736		5,736

John Horan
John Horan, Returning Officer

11 April 1981

Figure 20 Result

candidates, both nominated by FWUI, and 1 was elected – by transfers within her own union and from the only other "flight" candidate. She finally reached the quota with 190 votes transferred from the second woman but it is not possible to determine how many of these constituted a "women's vote".

In contrast to the General Medical Council, the poll was very high, 89 per cent, and with only 31 papers (0.5 per cent) invalid for all reasons. The difference may be due partly to familiarity with the voting system on the part of all except a small minority based outside Ireland, and to the very good publicity and instructions given in the airline's newspaper. Of the other six boards, five had polls between 76 and 97 per cent; the exception was the Electricity Supply Board with only 54 per cent. Its report says this "did reflect earlier trends in employee participation" and was connected with "the dispersed nature of employee location throughout the company". In all the boards, the trade unions and other sections obtained representation in close proportion to their voting strengths.

No other electoral system yet devised approaches "Supervote" in its capacity to reflect the voters' opinions about whatever they consider to be important in the circumstances of their particular election.

It should attract the attention of, among others, political parties suffering from dissention between their component parts. If the MPs, the annual conference, the national executive and the constituency organizations are in serious disagreement they cannot all be representative of grassroots opinion. The party's internal democratic machinery needs overhaul to ensure that all its elected bodies reflect the wishes of the membership.

10

Second Chambers

When the House of Lords, in WS Gilbert's words, "did nothing in particular and did it very well", it tended to be treated as "a source of innocent merriment" for the cartoonists. It appeared less harmless when obstructing Gladstone's Irish Home Rule bills, and ceased to be a joke when the Liberal government of 1906 found its reforming measures frustrated by the Lords. That government had not only a huge majority in the Commons but – for once – more than half the votes cast in that election and obvious popular support for such measures as the miners' eight-hour day. Opposition by the unelected house caused mounting resentment, culminating in a storm over the Lords' rejection of the "People's Budget" of 1909. Two general elections were fought on the issue of "Peers versus People" and the Parliament Act of 1911 removed all power of the Lords over money bills and, with regard to other bills, left them only a delaying power of two years. (Since reduced to one year and then to six months.)

This removed the House of Lords as a prominent object of attention until 1947, when the Labour government revived attacks on its undemocratic nature, denouncing it as a bastion of privilege. The main bone of contention is its permanent bias in favour of only one party, the Lords being relied upon to help a Conservative government and hinder a Labour one. Few would dispute that this is wrong, and there seems also to be general agreement that heredity ought not to confer automatically a right to legislate. Beyond that, however, there is little agreement. One important reform has been made, the creation of life peers under an Act of 1958. This has certainly made valuable additions to the personnel of that house (including two members who, with one hereditary peer, constitute the only ethnic minority representatives in either house) and has done something to correct the party imbalance, but there is pressure for further reform and the Labour left demands total abolition of the upper house.

In May 1981, in the most recent of many schemes of reform, Sir Brandon Rhys Williams, MP, sought to introduce under the ten-minute rule, a bill which would have retained the existing member-ship of the Lords but restricted voting power to about 250 additional members, elected by PR from the Euro-constituencies. This was rejected by 137 votes to 61, and was criticized as impracticable. Norman St John Stevas, MP, has put forward an alternative scheme, for a house composed of all the life peers, plus peers to the number of about one third of the whole, elected by PR, some of the hereditary peers, elected by them, and representatives of all the churches. There have been numerous proposals for introducing some elected element and most of these, if not all, assume proportional representation. But this would make the Lords more representative than the Commons. What then?

Most democracies do have a two-chamber parliament, but why? There are two different reasons. One is that the two houses are designed to represent different divisions of the nation. This is most clearly seen in the case of federations, where each state, province, canton or whatever it may be called is regarded as a unit with interests and opinions that need to be represented in the one house while those of the individual citizen are in the other. For elections to the United States' House of Representatives, each citizen is equal, whether he lives in a small state or a large one, but for elections to the Senate each state is equal, so that Vermont or Wyoming has its two spokesmen just like New York or California with twenty times as many people. A similar conception lies behind the Irish Senate, whose members are elected not directly by the people but by certain interests such as the universities or agriculture. The same idea accounts for the ex officio membership of 26 archbishops and bishops in the House of Lords, and is the basis of some proposals for reform of that institution.

The other useful function of the upper house is quite different: it is to act as a revising chamber, able to correct the faults of ill-considered bills, or to consider unhurriedly matters crowded out from the agenda of the overworked Commons. Up to a point, the House of Lords does perform these functions well. Many a subject is aired in the Lords by people with expert knowledge of it, and occasionally bills presented in the Commons are rejected or drastically amended by the Lords. An instance of this occurred at the end of 1976 during the passage of the Labour government's Aircraft and Shipbuilding Bill, designed to nationalize those industries. The Lords carried an amendment to remove ship repairing from the scope of the bill, and although the government threatened to re-introduce the bill, unamended, under the terms of the Parliament Act, it did not in fact do so but accepted the amended version. Possibly it was influenced in so doing by clear evidence that in another matter, being debated at the same time, the balance of public opinion was on the side of the Lords. The Dock Work Regulation Bill originally gave dockers the exclusive right to such work, not only within ports but up to five miles from them. A Lords amendment reduced the five miles to half a mile. When the bill came back to the Commons, the government found itself faced with protests from other trade unions and revolt by some of its own MPs, and gave way.

In these two cases the unelected chamber was correcting what the majority of the nation felt to be an error on the part of the elected chamber – and which would have gone uncorrected if the Lords had not existed. In other cases it might not be at all clear that this was so, and a Labour government could very reasonably accuse the predominantly Conservative peers of frustrating the will of the people's elected representatives. (It is precisely because their lord-ships feel their position in this respect to be weak that they seldom exercise their full power.) If a revising chamber is needed, it ought to be able to do its work impartially and not be held back by fear of being accused of bias even if the charge is baseless.

Hence the wide acceptance of the idea that elections to the upper house ought to be proportional. But proportional to what? To party strengths in the lower house? That would certainly minimize conflict between the two houses, but would seem to make the second one redundant. To party strengths in the country? That seems to be in the mind of many now urging reform, but if the House of Commons were still elected as now it would guarantee conflict most of the time. It would give the Lords greater moral authority than the Commons, as it has strengthened the power of the Australian Senate relative to the House of Representatives. And if the lower house also is reformed, will the upper house still be needed? Can it be rescued from the dilemma of the Abbé Sieyès: "If a second chamber dissents from the first, it is mischievous; if it agrees with it, it is superfluous"?

If the House of Commons is made truly representative, plainly the need for any check on its actions will be less. But it may still benefit from a second opinion, or from being told to stop and think again. The design of machinery for this purpose requires much further discussion, but a vital part of it will be a second chamber elected by STV, so as to enable the electors to choose men and women who represent all important interests and are well qualified to do so. A point frequently made in defence of the existing House of Lords is that its members often show much more independence than do MPs – even if they have previously been reliable cogs in a party machine – and more often than the Commons initiate discussion of unpopular subjects. This is because (like judges, who are appointed for life precisely in order to ensure their independence of undue influence) they no longer depend on their party for a seat in the next parliament. With STV, they depend instead on the free choice of their electors, who are likely to prefer a representative with courage and a mind of his own.

11

Why Not?

The Electoral Reform Society is nearing its centenary; all the major political parties have groups within them pressing for a change in the present British electoral system; since 1976 the National Campaign for Electoral Reform has been supporting their activities; all public opinion polls show majorities of around two to one in favour of a change; the number of organizations conducting their elections by the single transferable vote continues to increase rapidly – yet those who are in a position to change the law still cling obstinately to the existing system. Why?

An answer is difficult to find, for next to nothing is published which opposes reform by reasoned argument based on facts. The extent to which opposition arises from sheer ignorance – in quarters where one is entitled to expect adequate information – can be judged from the parliamentary debates on the bills for Scottish and Welsh assemblies and direct election of the European parliament. "Proportional representation inevitably leads in some form to coalitions." (Earl Ferrers, 4 April 1978; Hansard col. 87.) Tell that to the Tasmanians, who in over seventy years have not yet reached the inevitable. "Whichever form of proportional representation is selected, it means that more power and patronage is given to the party machines." (Douglas Jay, MP, 20 April 1977; Hansard, col. 226; and others.) The Irish evidently have not been informed of this, for their voters frequently override the party machines in a way the British cannot do. "With a two-party system, first-past-the-post is the most exactly proportional method that can be achieved." (Anthony Kershaw, MP, 23 November 1977; Hansard, col. 1561.) What about South Africa's two-party election in 1948, when a 5-to-4 vote for the one side gave a 5-to-4 majority of the contested seats to the other side? "The alternative vote system does not lead in Europe, and it would not lead here, to permanent minority government or coalition.' (George Reid, MP, 12 January 1978; Hansard, col. 1905.) The alternative vote has never been used in Europe. "Under the single transferable vote system ... there is no representative whom any constituent can hold uniquely responsible or accountable for anything to which that representative assents." (Enoch Powell, MP, 23 November 1977; Hansard, col. 1543.) Whyever not? Each constituent has one member to whose election he has contributed, and if that member acts contrary to his election promises the electors can turn him out next time; he is accountable directly to his constituents instead of to a party organization. "There is one fundamental objection to all forms of proportional representation ... that it means representation of parties, not of individuals." (Ivor Stanbrook, MP, 23 November 1977; Hansard col. 1576.) "*All* forms." Mr Stanbrook was evidently unaware that one form – the single transferable vote – is used in elections where no parties exist, and that even where they play a very important part the voters elect whichever individual candidates they wish – and quite often choose independents.

Failure to distinguish between STV and party list systems is one of the commonest errors, and arises from the omission of both our largest parties to give their members any adequate information on the subject. Even the generally admirable Conservative discussion brief* does not refer to the vital distinction between them (and is inaccurate in regard to the West German system). As for the Labour party, it has for many years published nothing that could help its members to argue intelligently either for or against any change in our present system.

Why should any party persist in exposing its spokesmen to the risk of making themselves look foolish in public, simply for lack of the information which they surely have a right to expect from their party's otherwise efficient information service? Until an honourable explanation is forthcoming, there must be a suspicion that the party knows the existing system to be indefensible but clings to it because it offers the party the prospect of a majority of seats without the need to convince a majority of the voters, and power to fill those seats with the men or women the party wants, whether or not they are those whom the voters want.

* *Electoral Reform and Devolution*, Contact Brief 66, Conservative Political Centre, January 1975.

Some of the objections raised to abandoning first-past-the-post are of a trifling nature or easily disproved by experience. When weeks have been spent on an election campaign, does it really matter if it takes a few hours extra to get the result right? When school-children can cope not only with voting 1, 2, 3 ... but with counting votes, can it seriously be suggested that adult British voters need stick to the illiterate's X?

There are, however, other objections raised which deserve much more serious consideration. The two important ones are the belief that strong government requires a parliamentary majority for one party, and resistance to the multi-member constituency.

STRONG GOVERNMENT

This is a complex question. The basic assumption is that a govern-ment must be assured, for the lifetime of a parliament, of power to carry out the whole programme on which it fought the election. That this is not the only way of governing a country successfully is shown most clearly by Switzerland, where such domination by a single party would be regarded as quite wrong. There are also signs that British electors are by no means so attached to this conception of strong government as are their politicians. The man-in-the-street often expresses the opinion that there is some good in all parties, and many, though not all, public opinion polls show strong support for coalition rather than one-party government. When the February 1974 election gave a House of Commons with no clear majority for any one party, a series of opinion polls showed very small demand for a fresh election and a large majority favouring either a continua-tion of the minority Labour government or a coalition of the three main parties.* Fear or dislike of coalition is felt not by the ruled but by the rulers, who naturally find life much easier if they know they can carry all their proposals and need not bow to criticism from outside their own party.

The argument about whether coalition is a good or a bad thing becomes confused with the argument about which electoral systems are likely to produce or prevent it, and – in the absence of sufficient publicity for the facts through the political parties and the news media – sweeping assertions like that of Earl Ferrers (p 156) are all

* *The Times*, 25 March 1974. Another election did take place the following October.

too common. Those who assert that because no one party has polled as much as half the votes in any election since the last war, therefore under PR Britain would have had perpetual coalitions all that time are naive. It assumes that, under a different electoral system, voters' support for the parties would have remained unchanged, and that is certainly untrue. For instance, to make the vote transferable would reduce, if not eliminate, the "tactical voting" that now takes place.

It is true that a system like the British, which frequently gives a single party a parliamentary majority for a minority of the votes, is less likely to produce coalitions than is one which ensures that no party can win more than half the seats unless backed by more than half the voters. But on the other hand any proportional system does mean that if a party succeeds in winning the support of more than half the voters it is certain of a parliamentary majority – while under the British system this is not a certainty, though a high probability. Even a small risk of a result like the South African in 1948 should not be accepted. In a "straight fight" the government, supported by more than half the voters, was defeated:

outgoing government's percentage of votes	51.4
outgoing government's percentage of contested seats won	43.5

It will presumably be agreed that if a party can win the support of at least half the voters it is entitled to form the government. Disagreement arises over what should be done if no single party is in that position. Supporters of the British electoral system commonly argue that it is necessary for strong and stable government that one party should be in a position to carry out the whole of its consistent programme and not be in constant danger of defeat on one item of it or another. But if this is of such importance as to justify overriding the wishes of the majority who have *not* voted for that party, is it not too important to be left to chance? Although British elections more often than not do give one party a working majority in the House of Commons, they have failed to do so in seven out of the 21 elections this century (in five of them no majority at all, in the other two a tiny and precarious one). If it is thought such a good thing that the largest party, with 48 per cent of the votes, should win two thirds of the seats, as happened in 1945 by the chances of the X-vote, would it not be better to make sure of such a result by copying Mussolini's law which awarded two thirds of the seats to the party with the most votes? At least that would have prevented the absurdity of the 1951 election, when the same party, with slightly *increased* support, was thrown out of office by the party with the second largest number of votes. Or we might give the prime minister (or the sovereign) power to appoint additional MPs to a number that would guarantee him a working majority.

Such suggestions are usually received as a joke, but if they are to be ruled out as frivolous what is the alternative? If we are not going to tamper with the result of an election, we must accept it as it is and make government work on that basis. British governments in the situation of having no working majority have usually managed it badly and been short lived, but even here we have had two exceptions, resulting from the elections of 1910. These left the Liberals with no majority on their own but dependent on Irish Nationalist (and/or Labour) support; this did not prevent them from carrying out a considerable programme of reform, including the curbing of the power of the House of Lords. The essential to success in such circumstances is to abandon the claim that a party has a mandate for every item in its manifesto and should resign if defeated, and accept instead that it will bow to the will of the House, leaving aside for the time being any of its cherished projects to which the majority will not consent.

This happens more easily under a proportional system, partly because any claim to a mandate by a party supported only by a minority is more obviously spurious when it has only a minority of the seats, and partly because there is less chance of running away from the problem. In Britain, a party trying to govern without a parliamentary majority is tempted to throw in its hand and call a new election, in the hope that this will either give it a working majority or relieve it of responsibility, but under a proportional system a small change in the voting such as is likely over a short period can produce only a small change in the parliament, so the parties must make the best of their situation. The commonest solution is a coalition of two or more parties that have been able to agree on a common programme, leaving aside items of their respective policies on which they disagree. Alternatively, as tends to happen in Denmark, one party may govern alone, so regulating its actions as always to command sufficient support from among the other parties.

All this applies to a country using any kind of proportional representation, but STV changes the position materially as compared with a party list system. To begin with, it is less likely to give rise to a situation in which a coalition is necessary, because it has a strong tendency to reduce the number of parties. (See especially Tasmania, p 81.) Secondly, STV places much less emphasis on opposition of one party to another, and enables supporters of different parties to express their agreements as well as their differences. By giving one candidate preference over another of the same party, and by voting on particular questions across the party lines, voters can show what policies most of them would like any government to pursue, and by voting 1, 2, 3 ... for candidates of Party A and then going on to those of Party B they can show that they consider those parties have much in common and should work together. In over sixty years, Ireland has had only three coalition governments (four if we include the Fine Gael government elected in 1981, which, though not explicitly a coalition, included four Labour ministers). They have been demonstrably the wish of the majority of the voters and have been formed very quickly, with little of the prolonged bargaining behind the scenes liable to go on when decisions on which party should combine with which rest solely in the hands of the party leaders, not in those of the people.

When it is claimed that the British electoral system produces strong and stable government, we need to ask just what is meant by those terms. Is a government strong if it has an unassailable parliamentary majority? If so, the government of our appeasement period must be accounted the strongest in our history. A parliamentary majority plus a prime minister who knows her own mind and will not be diverted from the course she believes to be right may reasonably be called strength, but is that strength enhanced by the knowledge that the people whose car stickers proclaim that they did not vote for that government represent the majority of the nation? If a government has come to power with the support of at least half the voters, its moral authority must be greater.

A related argument is that if no one party has more than half the seats, government is actually in the hands, not of a majority, but of a small party in a balancing position, able by bargaining with the larger parties to decide which of them takes office. This, however, is generally put forward as a theory, seldom backed by concrete instances. Does anyone maintain that the British government of 1910–15 was an Irish Nationalist one? Because the small Free Democratic party has formed part of nearly every West German government, have those governments pursued FDP policies? Even under a party list system, where coalition-building does depend on bargaining between party leaders, it is difficult to see how a small party can impose on the country any policy peculiar to itself and opposed unitedly by the larger parties, i.e. by the majority. In any case, even if the power of a balancing party is a real danger, it is far less dangerous than the power that may be wielded under the British system by far smaller minorities. In 1967 the Sikh community in Britain voted £25,000 a year to set up its own political party and a headquarters in London. It estimated that the community, numbering about 100,000, could decide the election result in a dozen marginal constituencies. As it happened, the next election was won by the Conservatives with a margin of 30 seats over all other parties combined, so in that instance the Sikh vote could not have been decisive (which is perhaps why nothing further has been heard publicly about this plan). However, in the following election, February 1974, things were far otherwise. Labour won the most seats (with fewer votes than the Conservatives) but not a clear majority, and no less than 72 MPs were elected by "majorities" of less than 2,000 – 37 of them Labour, 28 Conservative and 7 others. Therefore those 100,000 Sikhs, by changing sides, could quite easily have either given Labour a clear majority of the seats or put the Conservatives in power instead. Indeed, for all we know, the actual result may have been brought about by some well-organized pressure group, whether an ethnic minority, nuclear disarmers, the Lord's Day Observance Society, or anything else. One hundred thousand people are well over the average electorate of one constituency and therefore have a reasonable claim to representation by one MP, but they are not entitled to decide the government of the whole forty million electors. Under a proportional system, a very small number of voters changing sides will have only a correspondingly small effect.

Not only are the voters who decide the result of a close British election very few compared with the numbers likely to have supported a balancing party, they are also (in the literal sense) irresponsible. They may have changed sides for the most sound and serious reasons or for foolish ones; no one even knows, and they are answerable to nobody. The balancing party, on the contrary, gives its support to one side or another openly and, if it tries to abuse its power, can be punished by the voters in the next election.

As for stability, that may mean the stability of a single government which has an assured parliamentary majority and cannot be forced out of office before the end of its legal term. Stability in this sense may be achieved more often under a system which tends to give one party an exaggerated majority of seats, and a split leading to the downfall of the government may be less likely in a single disciplined party than in a coalition. (Whether stability in this sense is a good or a bad thing in the case of an unpopular government is another question.) However, stability may also be thought of as applying to a period of time much longer than the life of one parliament, and in this sense there is no doubt at all that proportional representation in general, and the single transferable vote in particular, tend to produce gradual evolution rather than drastic change, lasting development rather than repeated reversals of policy.

> Investment is always risky, but the risks in the United Kingdom are quite unnecessarily enhanced by the impossibility of predicting what government attitudes will be in 5 years' time on anything from tax to worker participation to import controls, let alone in the 15 to 20 years which it might require to recover one's investment and make a reasonable profit on it.
>
> Maurice Zinkin, *The Guardian*, 22 July 1981

That is an important reason why so many industrialists and businessmen have been seeking a change in the British electoral system, and it applies equally to those who invest their brains in schools, hospitals or any other institution that is seriously affected by government policy. The present Conservative government has returned to private hands parts of the nationalized industries and the Labour party conference of 1980 announced that when that party regained power it would re-nationalize them without compensation. How many are willing to invest under such conditions? It is easy to make a case for nationalizing an industry or for leaving it to private enterprise; for preserving a grammar school or for merging it in a comprehensive system; but no one can point to any advantage to the nation or to the people directly concerned in switching from the one policy to the other and back again and never knowing what the position will be after the next general election.

Should shipbuilding be nationalized? Should all schools be comprehensive? Should private practice in medicine be allowed? On any one of such questions there will be a majority of electors saying either yes or no, and it is unlikely that this majority will reverse itself over a short period, still more unlikely that it will sway back and forth repeatedly every few years. So if we want the industrialist, the head teacher, the hospital administrator and so forth to be able to plan ahead over a reasonable length of time, it will suffice to find out which policy is favoured by the majority and stick to it until such time as the majority changes its mind. In Britain, this is not happening because (a) the ruling party does not have even the general support of the majority of those voting; (b) there is nothing in the election to show which of its policies in particular do have majority support; (c) the ruling party nevertheless claims a mandate for all of them, and (d) when a different party takes office this in its turn claims a mandate to reverse the previous government's measures.

Any form of proportional representation will remedy this situation as far as (a) is concerned. If it gives rise to a coalition, or to a one-party minority government, it will tend also to prevent the passage of measures that do not command majority support and to make permanent those which do, since the smaller party or parties will support those of the largest party which they share, but refuse to vote for those with which they disagree. The position will tend towards that characteristic of the Scandinavian countries, where an idea that may have originated in any one of the parties wins general acceptance and survives many changes of government. The single transferable vote is a still greater stabilizing force, because it gives the voters a *direct* influence on the adoption or rejection of any policy about which they feel strongly. In France in 1981 the Socialists polled more than half the total votes and therefore would still have come to power if a proportional system had been in force (provided the same number of voters supported them). The new government is committed to a published list of 21 reforms* and it cannot be assumed that all those who voted Socialist, or all the Socialist candidates, agree with the whole 21. For instance there may be some, perhaps many, who welcome "administrative structural reform giving more power to regions" but object to "nationalization of 11 industrial groups". Or vice versa. If election had been by STV, Socialist voters would have been able to give preference to those Socialist candidates who shared their opinions on these matters and thus to ensure a parliamentary majority for those of the 21 promises (and only those) which had majority support among the voters. They would also have been able to show which candidates of other parties they agreed with on certain points. This last is of great importance for the framing and sustaining of an agreed programme, for it contributes to a co-operative spirit and does away with having

---

* See *The Times*, 10 July 1981.

to vote as if we thought our own side was perfect and all others were enemies.

"No government which is in a large minority in the country, even though it possesses a working majority in the House of Commons, can have the necessary power to cope with real problems."* The moral authority of any government must be strengthened if everyone can see that it came to power with the consent of the majority.

LARGE CONSTITUENCIES

The other objection which holds a certain amount of water is the dislike of large, multi-member constituencies. It must be conceded that, other things being equal, most people would prefer a small constituency to a large one and most MPs (though probably not their constituents) would prefer to be the sole representative of their constituency rather than share it with others. But other things are very far from equal.

To begin with, whatever disadvantages the multi-member constituency may have, it is essential to secure anything like proportional representation. With election in single-member constituencies only, it is impossible to ensure even that the party with the most votes will win the most seats.† The West German system does indeed retain single-member constituencies, but only at the cost of "topping-up" from constituencies returning up to 75 members each. The variants of this system that are being put forward in the United Kingdom similarly – and necessarily – involve pooling votes over a large area. It is difficult to understand why people who attach such importance to the link between one MP and his constituents accept so readily the creation of other MPs who have no such link. One proposed variation does indeed assign an additional MP (or perhaps two) to a particular single-member constituency, but why is that more acceptable than making it a two- or three-member constituency in the first place? It would still, of course, be smaller than the constituencies necessary to give reasonably fair representation (five or so members), but it would destroy what is claimed to be the unique personal relationship between the one MP and the entire electorate for whom he is solely responsible.

How real is that relationship in fact? A Conservative lady, who

* Winston Churchill.
† See p 21.

clearly did feel closely linked to the Conservative MP whom she had helped to elect, knew personally and admired, was asked how she would react if she lived in the constituency of a left-wing Labour MP. "I'd move!" she said. But there are thousands of Conservatives who do live in that constituency, thousands of Socialists who live under a right-wing Conservative, and neither can really think of him as *their* MP. It is true that any British MP, with very rare exceptions, can be relied on to serve all his constituents, without distinction of party, when they come to him with personal problems, but with the best will in the world he cannot be of any service to the constituent who is seeking to promote a cause contrary to the policy of the MP and his party. And it is precisely these latter questions which determine how we vote. Very few choose the candidate they think most likely to be helpful about the nuisance next door or the disappearance of a bus service; most vote for the candidate of the party we most nearly agree with on the big questions of government policy. Some MPs are certainly aware that their personal contacts do not by any means extend to all their constituents.

I believe the myth of the single-member constituency being of special value is best tackled by vigorous advocacy of the benefit to the constituent of having several MPs representing the same constituency. Since I was first elected in 1966, I have been well aware that a significant number of constituents are most unlikely to approach me personally except perhaps in the direst emergency. They imagine, rightly or wrongly, that a person of my age, sex and background will not understand their problem, or that I will not advocate what they want. It seems to me quite wrong that they should only have one MP to turn to, rather than a choice. I am afraid that the imagined advantages of the single-member constituency have been propagated ... without sufficient contradiction.

Richard Wainwright, MP
letter, 22 July 1981

Another Liberal MP, David Penhaligon of Truro, finds a great contrast between his postbag and that of the Conservative representing the adjoining, and very similar, constituency – indicating that each is approached not by a cross-section of all his constituents, but predominantly by those of his own party.

How serious are the drawbacks of much larger constituencies? They cannot be fatal, for constituencies far larger than any proposed for the House of Commons already operate successfully. To take an extreme example, New South Wales is one STV constituency for Senate elections; it has six times the area of all England and twice the population of Wales. An MP for one of the divisions of Buckinghamshire may be horrified by the idea of the whole county as one constituency, meaning that if he lives at one end of the county and wishes to meet a constituent at the other end, one or other of them must travel fifty miles each way. But any of the five Deputies for Co Wexford is in the same position, and nobody complains that he is out of touch with his constituents.

Whatever the disadvantages of size, as regards personal contact, they are far outweighed by the advantages. To begin with, the act of voting by STV is far more personal: the voter can no longer vote just for a party but (at least in the case of the larger parties) must decide which of its candidates he prefers to the others. Nearly every voter finds himself with a representative whom he has actually helped to elect – at least one of the party he favours and, in most cases, also a man or woman whom he prefers to other candidates of that party – and whom at the next election he can either re-elect or reject according to whether he considers him to have given good or bad service. Every Irish Deputy is in the position of a British MP for a highly marginal constituency, obliged to nurse his constituency lest the loss of a few personal votes lose him the seat next time; none can be tempted to neglect it as an MP may be in a seat safe for his party. The member with a high reputation is very unlikely to lose his seat, for if his party suffers a setback the members it loses will be those least esteemed by the voters. There is sometimes advanced the rather childish objection that an elector with several MPs will not know which of them to approach with his problem. Most of us have several local councillors; does that prevent anybody from seeking the help of one of them? Usually, an elector will apply to the member he has helped to elect, but he is not obliged to do so; he may prefer to call on one who lives near, or on one known to have a special interest in the matter involved. All the members for his constituency are equally at his service. And they are the more likely to be able to serve him well because they will almost certainly be local men or women, well acquainted with local problems and, even before they became candidates, better known to the people of that large constituency than any of them could be to a small part of it if he came from the other end of the country. Under the present British system a large number of MPs have no roots in the constituencies they purport to represent – because, for instance, a Labour supporter living in Surrey or a Conservative in Co Durham has virtually no hope of ever representing his own home in parliament, while if each migrates to the other's home he can have a sage seat. Under a proportional system (even an impersonal party list) such a person can stay in the area he knows and represent the minority there.

On the other hand, that member's interests will be less parochial. The larger constituency is sure to contain a variety of occupations and life styles, preventing the MP from becoming identified too exclusively with any one of them. Multi-member constituencies have some positive advantages, especially the avoidance of frequent revisions, liable to have serious effects on the result of an election, and the openings they offer to people unlikely to be selected as a party's sole candidate anywhere.*

If the arguments against proportional representation in general and the single transferable vote in particular are no more substantial than this, must we seek other motives for the opposition consistently shown by governments of different party complexions? It is to be feared that one motive is revealed by the speech of a Labour MP and by Conservative ones to similar effect: "I am certain that in this country we would not achieve the Socialist society that I want to create by a system of PR and coalition governments".† The MP is opposing PR on the ground that it would not give power to the party he thinks ought to have power. But why wouldn't it? If the majority of voters support that party, PR will ensure that it gets a majority in the House of Commons; we can only *not* get Socialism if the majority do *not* want it. So what speeches like this amount to is:

> I know most of you don't agree with me but I'm sure my idea of good government is right, so I cling to an electoral system which gives a good chance of imposing it on you against your will; a system that offers *my* party the prospect of a majority of seats without needing to convince a majority of the voters, and power to fill those seats with the men and women the party wants, whether or not they are the ones the voters want.

Is this a libel on the people concerned? If so, it is to be hoped that they will produce some more honourable reasons for their adherence to X-voting and show more readiness to discuss alternatives to it.

* See p 136.
† Alexander Lyon, MP, 13 December 1977; Hansard, col. 382.

12

In Your Hands

Among the conditions that may entitle a country to be called a democracy are two. That every citizen is free to express his own opinions and endeavour to persuade others to share them, and that those who can persuade only a minority must not impose their views on the majority. The British electoral system manages to violate both conditions.

It is notorious that nearly all British governments, and a large number of those elected abroad under the same system, come to power with the support of less than half of those who vote. What is not so obvious is that a minority, including the minority forming the government, may be inhibited from putting its case honestly to the electors. Take for instance a person on the left of the Labour party, who is convinced that the party is betraying its socialist ideals and ought to be pursuing a far more radical policy of public owner-ship. He has a right, and indeed a duty, to say so, but if his party is to have a chance of putting such a policy into effect it must win an election. That requires attracting millions of voters, while alienating as few as possible, and the party leaders will be well aware of public opinion polls which consistently show those left-wing policies to be unpopular. So people of "extreme" opinions likely to frighten off voters must be persuaded to play them down. Until the election is safely won.

It does not follow that the "extreme" policies will not be put into effect, for it may well happen that their advocates will have managed to get themselves selected as candidates for most of the winnable seats and so to dominate the parliamentary party. Behind the scenes manipulation of a party's machinery may be far more effective than open advocacy of a cause. The British electoral system can hinder the expression of unpopular opinions, while facilitating their imposition on the majority who disagree.

It does so by depriving the *voters* of means to express their opinion on particular questions, while causing their votes to be taken as total support for the whole package of policies presented by one party or another. The single transferable vote form of PR will reverse this, bringing the position much nearer to what honest people would wish it to be. A person of extreme or unorthodox opinions will no longer need to conceal them but can honestly seek votes for them. A party need not try to prevent his candidature, for he will do no harm if included in a team with the more moderate and orthodox – any voters who dislike his extremism will just ignore him and give preference to the moderates. If – and only if – the extremists can persuade the majority of voters that they are right, they will secure a parliamentary majority. If not, they may get a few spokesmen in the Commons, but no more than their popular support warrants.

Under STV, the MP is rendered accountable directly to his constituents, who have chosen him personally and who, in the next election, can either reaffirm that choice or alter it. There is therefore no chance that an MP elected on certain pledges will go against them on the orders of a party whip; to do so would be to invite defeat next time at the hands of those who elected him. Intrigues to pack a party with candidates of a particular complexion cannot succeed, for those of different views can insist on nominating others – there being no longer any risk of splitting the party's vote – and the voters will elect whichever they prefer.

Power passes into the hands of the voters, and so of course does responsibility. It is a far bigger change than is generally realized, even by those already convinced of the need for it.

While large majorities declare themselves in favour of changing the British electoral system to one reflecting more fairly the voters' opinions, relatively few give this a high place in their list of things that need doing. Work for the unemployed, homes for the homeless, a check to ever-rising prices, salvation from the threat of nuclear war – all such matters appear far more important than the machinery of elections. But they all involve the government, parliament or perhaps the local authority, and how are electors to get the action they want if their votes do not control those bodies? At present the Briton, by his vote, cannot even *say* what he wants, let alone have any assurance of getting it. He may, for example, be desperately anxious to reverse the existing government's policy on unemployment, and therefore vote for a party with the opposite policy. But he then finds that his vote has been counted also as endorsing that party's policy on, say, nuclear weapons, to which he may be strongly opposed. Or perhaps none of the local candidates may be prepared to commit himself to the particular cause the voter has at heart. And if there is such a candidate he may be an independent or the champion of some tiny party that seems to have not the remotest chance of winning. In that case the voter may well abandon the opportunity of expressing his real opinion and use his vote simply to keep out the candidate or the party he thinks is the worst.

The electors who have in fact so little power to elect must cease to put up with their position. With celebrations of 150 years since the first Reform Act began the march towards a vote for every adult, we must advance to a vote that really elects. What stands in the way? Legislators who owe their position to the existing system, and who for the most part have insufficient information to put up a convincing argument either for it or for any alternative. Fortunately, increasing numbers of them have doubts and are becoming open to pressure from constituents who have mastered essential facts. Elections are for the people, not the parties, and it is for the people to assert their right to elect – not merely to vote.

The Times of 28 May 1862 complained of the annual waste of parliamentary time on a "crazy old question" which had "had its day". "It may continue to furnish an annual subject for an eccentric member to dilate upon, but ... the idea that a Bill will pass the House of Commons enters into the mind of no one."

A Bill on what? The secret ballot. Ten years later, it had become law. To our descendants it may seem equally strange that so sane a measure as PR/STV should ever have been opposed.

Bibliography

Bogdanor, Vernon, *The People and the Party System*, Cambridge University Press, 1981.

British Council of Churches, *Report on Electoral Reform*, 1982.

Butler, David E, *The Electoral System in Britain, 1918–1951*, Oxford University Press, 1952.

    With other authors, *The British General Election of 1945* and subsequent elections.

Campbell, Peter, *French Electoral Systems and Elections since 1789*, Faber and Faber, 1958.

Carstairs, Andrew, *Comparative Electoral Systems in Western Europe*, George Allen and Unwin, 1980.

Cook, Chris and Ramsden, John, *By-elections in British Politics*, Macmillan, 1973.

Craig, FWS, *British Parliamentary Election Statistics, 1918–1968*, Political Reference Publications, Glasgow, 1968.

Finer, SE (Ed), *Adversary Politics and Electoral Reform*, Anthony Wigram, 1975.

Holt, Stephen, *Six European States; the Countries of the European Community and their Political Systems*, Hamish Hamilton, 1970.

Howatt, George, *Democratic Representation under the Hare-Clark System*, Government Printer, Hobart, 1958.

    Fixing Responsibility for Governing, when no party has an absolute majority in parliament, Government Printer, Hobart, 1960.

Kermode, DG, *Devolution at Work; a case study of the Isle of Man*, Saxon House, 1979.

Knight, James, *Northern Ireland, the Elections of 1973*, Arthur McDougall Fund, 1974.

    Northern Ireland, the Election of the Constitutional Convention, May 1975, Arthur McDougall Fund, 1975.

    with Nicolas Baxter-Moore, *Northern Ireland, the Elections of the Twenties*, Arthur McDougall Fund, 1972.

    Republic of Ireland, the General Elections of 1969 and 1973, Arthur McDougall Fund, 1973.

Lakeman, Enid, *Nine Democracies; Electoral Systems of the Countries of the European Economic Community*, Arthur McDougall Fund, 1978.

Newland, Robert A, *Comparative Electoral Systems*, Arthur McDougall Fund, 1982.

Pugh, Martin, *Electoral Reform in War and Peace, 1906–18*, Routledge and Keegan Paul, 1978.

Rogaly, Joe, *Parliament for the People*, Temple Smith, 1976.

Ross, JFS, *Parliamentary Representation*, Eyre and Spottiswoode, 1948.
The Irish Election System, Pall Mall Press, 1959.
The Achievement of Parliamentary Democracy, Aneurin Williams memorial lecture, Bowes and Bowes, 1952.

Royal Commission on Systems of Election, report and minutes of evidence, 1910.

Royal Commission on the Constitution, report, 1973.

Sasse, Christoph and others, *Das Wahlrecht der Neun*, Nomos Verlag, Baden-Baden, 1979.

Vallance, Elizabeth, *Women in the House*, Athlone Press, 1979.

Wilson, Alec, *PR Urban Elections in Ulster, 1920*, Electoral Reform Society, 1972.

Wright, JFH, *Mirror of the Nation's Mind; Australia's Electoral Experiments*, Hale and Iremonger, Sydney, 1980.

Index